# Focus on Acting

## Foundation

**'The Carne Method'**

By Robert Carne

*Robert Carne*

First Published lulu.com 2010
Adaptation from the Home Acting Course first published
Schemactor Pty Ltd 2001


Copyright © Schemactor Pty Ltd 2010
PO Box 36 Gladesville, 1675, NSW,
Australia
www.focusonacting.com
ISBN **978-1-4461-8527-8**


All rights reserved. No part of this publication may be
reproduced, stored in a retrieval system or transmitted in
any form or by any means, electrical, mechanical,
photocopying, recording or otherwise, without the prior
permission of the author.

Cover Design - Linde Davis
Back Cover Photo - Ben Symon

*Dedicated to Emma Ball*

*Robert Carne*

# Contents

Foreword ............................................................................................... 13
Preface .................................................................................................. 17
   *Using this Book* ............................................................................ 18
   *About the Author* ......................................................................... 18
   *Acknowledgments* ........................................................................ 18

CHAPTER 1 ........................................................................................ 21
  Conceptual Introductions ............................................................. 21
   *Introduction* .................................................................................. 22
   *Components of Acting* ................................................................. 22
   *What makes up a Production?* ................................................... 24
   *Choices* ......................................................................................... 27
   *Choices and Decision Making* .................................................... 28
   *How do we go about changing an Initial emotion?* ................. 34
   *Primary Cognition* ....................................................................... 34
   *Tertiary Cognition* ....................................................................... 35
   *Tips for Learning in the Classroom* ........................................... 38
   *Practical Exercises* ...................................................................... 41

CHAPTER 2 ........................................................................................ 45
  The Interaction ............................................................................... 45
   *Stages of Interaction* ................................................................... 46
   *Interaction in Motion* .................................................................. 67
   *Sub-Interactions* .......................................................................... 72
   *Interaction Model Summary* ...................................................... 73
   *Practical Exercises* ...................................................................... 74

CHAPTER 3 ........................................................................................ 75
  Behaviourism, Trust & Sociological Spheres of Influence ........ 75
   *Behaviorism* ................................................................................. 76
   *Causal Chains* .............................................................................. 78
   *Operant Conditioning* ................................................................. 79
   *Trust* ............................................................................................. 81
   *Transference of Effect* ................................................................ 86
   *Sociological Spheres of Influence* .............................................. 88
   *Emotionally Charged Props* ....................................................... 91
   *Practical Exercises* ...................................................................... 93

CHAPTER 4 .................................................................................. 95
  Vulnerability and Status.......................................................... 95
    *Vulnerability* ........................................................................ 96
    *Vulnerability Traits* ............................................................ 96
    *When Two Continuums Collide* ....................................... 106
    *Vulnerability History* ....................................................... 108
    *Status*.................................................................................. 110
    *Manipulating Status* ......................................................... 114
    *Practical Exercises* ........................................................... 124

CHAPTER 5 ................................................................................ 127
  Personal Space & Focus......................................................... 127
    *Personal Space*.................................................................. 128
    *What makes up our Personal Space?* ................................ 131
    *Personal Space Origins* .................................................... 132
    *Manipulating Personal Space* ........................................... 138
    *Proximetrics* ...................................................................... 141
    *The Seven Areas of Personal Space* ................................. 142
    *Practical Exercises* ........................................................... 152

CHAPTER 6 ................................................................................ 155
  Memory, Behaviour and the Script ....................................... 155
    *Memory* .............................................................................. 156
    *Encoding Specificity*......................................................... 156
    *Line Memorization* ........................................................... 158
    *Rules of Memorization* ..................................................... 162
    *Rules of Speed Runs* ......................................................... 166
    *Behaviour*........................................................................... 168
    *Vocal Behavior*.................................................................. 171
    *Visualization for Character Recall* ................................... 172
    *Recounting the Memory* ................................................... 179
    *Script Analysis* .................................................................. 180
    *Intellectualizing Meaning in the Script*............................. 181
    *Rehearsal and Performance Thresholds*........................... 184
    *Practical Exercises* ........................................................... 184

## CHAPTER 7 .................................................................................... 187
### Preparation and Recovery ........................................................ 187
*Preparation* ............................................................................ 188
*Vocal Warm-Up* .................................................................... 193
*Emotional Preparation* ......................................................... 198
*Phrase Prepping* ................................................................... 200
*Intellectual Preparation* ....................................................... 201
*Emotionally Charging Props* ............................................... 202
*Recovery* ............................................................................... 204
*Intellectual Method for Recovery* ........................................ 205
*The Thought Vault* ............................................................... 206
*Practical Exercises* .............................................................. 206

## CHAPTER 8 .................................................................................... 207
### Putting it all Together .............................................................. 207
*Introduction* ......................................................................... 208
*The Script* ............................................................................. 208
*Character History* ................................................................ 208
*Causal Chains* ..................................................................... 209
*Sociological Spheres of Influence* ....................................... 211
*Trust* ..................................................................................... 212
*Vulnerability* ........................................................................ 212
*Personal Space* .................................................................... 213
*Items* ..................................................................................... 214
*Status* .................................................................................... 215
*Interaction* ........................................................................... 216
*Learn Your Lines* .................................................................. 217
*Research* ............................................................................... 218
*Script Analysis* ..................................................................... 218
*Preparation* .......................................................................... 218
*Chapters Interacting* ........................................................... 219
*Things to Remember* ............................................................ 220
*Final Words* ......................................................................... 221
*Thank you* ............................................................................ 223
*Practical Exercises* .............................................................. 223

## Appendix A ..................................................................................... 225
### Sanford Meisner's Repetition Exercise ................................... 225
*Primary Function* ................................................................ 225
*The Repetition in Action* ...................................................... 227
*Taking the Repeat into Performance* ................................... 227

# Foreword

By John L Simpson

Acting... Craft or God given talent?

There is a lot of discussion and focus on talent in the public domain but for those who have made the commitment to become a professional actor, or those professionals who want to grow as artists the only **productive**, relevant label is craft.

One of the great myths expounded by those who view acting as purely an Art form is that "you either have it or you don't"... like many myths that statement is only half true, like any Art your ability as a practitioner improves with the application of knowledge and practice. Try telling a concert pianist it's all about talent... how about the eight hours a day of practice year after year? They ply their craft relentlessly so that the Art may flourish.

Do you have what it takes to be a successful actor? Do you have talent? Do you have enough talent to "make it?"

Relax... these questions are simply judgments made by others, they have no intrinsic worth, they are questions born of fear, fear of failure, fear of ridicule, fear of not being good enough... These questions do not reflect anything that has any bearing on whether or not you will succeed as an actor. The only real question worth asking yourself is, "do I want to be an actor?"

If your answer to this question is yes then studying Focus on Acting will definitely bring you closer to your goal of being an actor.

Robert Carne is a professional actor, director, writer and acting teacher. Drawing on his many years of professional experience, Carne has crafted this acting course with great intuition, affection and knowledge of what emerging actors need to know. Like a distilled essential oil, Carne gives you the "good stuff". He lays down the main foundations, covering human psychology, physicality, interaction, character creation, rehearsal technique and shares very important advice about professional practice.

Using his astute perception, Carne explains each concept in straight forward language with examples drawn from everyday life. The reader will no doubt have many "Eureka" moments as they read and re-read each chapter. Carne's many years of teaching experience shines through as he takes complex psychological concepts and breaks them down into easy to digest pieces. His tone differs from many acting texts as he writes without imposing his own ego on the text. There is always a strong sense that he is crafting it with the emerging actor in mind.

Robert Carne's Focus on Acting lays down a solid foundation upon which emerging actors may build their own technique and method of acting. Many acting schools are wary of those who have had previous training fearing they will have learnt bad habits or poor techniques that will be hard work to "undo". Focus on Acting has been specifically crafted to be complimentary to other acting methods and does not prescribe only one method but embraces many techniques, acknowledging that each of us learns in a different way.

Carne's "Focus on Acting" is a much needed and welcomed addition to the actor's tool kit and will no doubt be embraced by acting schools and actors alike for many years to come.

**John L Simpson - Producer - CEO TITAN VIEW**

John L is an award winning creative producer with over twenty five years experience working in the performing arts arena.

As an Actor John L worked professionally in internationally acclaimed productions such as: Sweeney

Todd, Les Miserables, The Phantom of the Opera, Into the Woods and Blood Brother.

John L began producing at the Melbourne Fringe Festival in 1992 with the critically acclaimed theatrical production, "My black heart – memories of apartheid". John L has Directed and Produced numerous Theatrical production since.

John's film productions have been screened at film festivals all over the world inc: Montreal, Palm Springs, Sydney, LA, Melbourne, London, Edinburgh, Algarve, Warsaw, Copenhagen, Rotterdam, Singapore, Martha's Vineyard…

John L launched 'TITAN VIEW' feature film distribution to bring important Australian films to Australian and international audiences. TITAN VIEW's first film for distribution was The Jammed, which was the highest grossing independent Australian film on screen average EVER, during its opening two weeks. The Jammed went on to win Best Film, Best Script and Best Score at the Inside Films Awards 2007.

In 2008 The United Nations selected The Jammed to be screened at an international conference on human trafficking in Vienna.

# Preface

Thank you for purchasing Focus on Acting - the *'Carne Method'*. The journey you are about to embark on may change the way you think, behave and interact with people forever. But most importantly it will give you an acting foundation that could see you achieving your greatest aspirations. So, what lies ahead?

For an actor to truly embrace the art I believe they must get to know themselves very well. Get to know their loves, their desires, their strengths, weaknesses, fears, hopes, vulnerabilities, their intimate emotional core - know them, accept them, love them. In this journey of discovery there comes a point when the actor can honestly look at themselves and realize that they intrinsically hold the potential for infinite other selves and that each of those selves are a part of their own 'self'. It is at this point, when we become `self-less', that we cease to judge others behavior and start to see past the shell of social parries and into the heart and soul of their inner life. We see their loves, their desires, their strengths, weaknesses, fears, hopes, vulnerabilities, their intimate emotional core and we can know them, accept them, love them. *Now* the actor may honestly and truthfully portray a character without judgment, without prejudice, without apology.

Humanity has infinite qualities that the arts seek to explore. In my humble opinion the art of acting reaches into the core of humanity and examines it as no other art form can. It allows an audience to see themselves in a light that would not normally be possible, it allows society to take stock of itself, it allows differing people who happen to exist at the same point in time to see their moment in eternity - together. To see the nature of existence and recognize their part in it.

Focus on Acting gets right down to the nuts and bolts of human interaction. This book is designed as a foundation template that you may incorporate other methods into, a holistic approach that gives you a unique acting and behavioral base that will evolve with you throughout your career.

## *Using this Book*

Firstly take your time with this book. No rush. The reason I say this is that the passing of time allows you to live with the ideas presented. You need time to absorb them, think about them, make them a part of you.

Resist the urge to read or skip ahead in Chapters. Take your time; enjoy the journey as I've set it out for you. Enjoy.

## *About the Author*

Robert Carne, born and raised in Sydney Australia, started acting in shows at 9 years of age. Not content with blindly accepting traditional acting method on faith, set out to discover for himself a way of acting, and coaching actors, that worked for him and was reproducible. With a University Degree from UNE Armidale majoring in Psychology & Drama, Robert started formulating his ideas which were to evolve over the years through acting, training and coaching actors. In 2001 Robert wrote the "Home Acting Course" which has to date been sold in over a dozen countries around the world. This book contains much of that course as well as new elements that have evolved.

## *Acknowledgments*

I appeared in my first show, outside of school, at the age of nine and started formal classes at twelve years of age. Since then I have had numerous teachers and directors, read many books and taught thousands of students all of whom I have learnt so much from. The contents of this book are a result of a cauldron of experiences that I have had over the years. Many ideas presented within have an amalgam of source inspirations and many are drawn from my observations and contemplations in life. It would be impossible for me to list all the influences that have contributed to this 'method' for, to be honest, what may have seemed to be spontaneous inspiration to me one day may have had a source in a long forgotten class. This book is truly my own evolution, the inspirations that have played upon me are too numerous to remember. However… I would like to formally acknowledge the work of a number of people whom I do remember and have definitely played some part in my development as an actor and in turn the information contained within.

Acting coaches, listed in no particular order;
Max Rowley, Grant Fickel, Malcolm Frawley, Carrie Zivetz, Bill Levis, Geoff Bourney, Egil Kipste, Adam McCauley, Eugene Buica, Veronique Bernard, Anthony Meindl, Jonathan Kehoe, Peter Pitcher, Launt Thompson, and Mariette Rups Donnelly.

Other influences include Constantin Stanislavski, Sanford Meisner, Sonia Moore, and Keith Johnson. I have read numerous acting texts at university as well as Psychology texts which undoubtedly all contributed to my cauldron of ideas.

I would like to acknowledge David Barnes, a friend of mine who was a sounding board for me when I was throwing ideas around about the relationship of vulnerability and status.

I'd also like to acknowledge Rob Lang and Cumberland Gang Show, ADASA, ACTT, all my Drama and Psychology lecturers at UNE Armidale and my fellow acting students in the numerous classes I have attended over the years.

My warmest thanks to John L Simpson for your friendship, advice and industry chats over the years and for agreeing to pen the Foreword, of which I am most grateful.

    I'd like to acknowledge my students, all of whom have meant a great deal to me. I particularly would like to thank my Sydney Teenage Actor's Studio students and also my Dance Action, MacArthur Performing Arts, Janice Breen, Wesley College, The Creative School and my wonderful Tuesday night students. I hope you learnt as much from me as I did from you.

    I must acknowledge the person who came up with the four stages of surprise, a theory upon which the Five Stages of Interaction are based. I have no idea who you are but thank you.

    If in the above I have missed someone with whom I have trained or studied with please accept my apologies. I am most grateful to all the influences in my life and though you may not have come immediately to mind, know that is it more a reflection of my memory than of your influence.

# CHAPTER 1

# *Conceptual Introductions*

**An Overview**

## Introduction

From the start I would like to point out that 'good Acting' is very 'individually specific' in its creation process. There is no right or wrong way to act, even though there is good and bad acting. What works for one actor may not work for another. There is no single answer to what makes an actor great or one single method that spawns great acting.

Great actors became great by finding that unique method of working that ignites their own individual creative spark. They have not merely learnt a method and put it into practice, they have learnt a method, or a number of methods, that they have internalized and then tailored to suit their own needs. All great actors are still learning. It is in the journey of discovery that keeps the actor fresh, it is in the journey of discovery that keeps the actor in the 'now'.

Focus on Acting the *'Carne Method'* is meant to be a foundation on which to build. While a complete method unto itself, it is ultimately the starting point, not the destination. I have met numerous actors that have trained for many years without ever solidifying a foundation on which to build, a base to go back to when things get tough. Focus on Acting will give you that solid base upon which you can create your own style of acting, a base which you don't have to toss aside every-time you have a new acting coach. The *'Carne Method'* provides the foundations for your own unique and evolving method of acting.

All theories contained within this book, are just that, theories, and I make no reference to them holding any universal truth. They are, however, very effective tools that I'm sure you'll find exceedingly useful in your journey to becoming a great actor.

## Components of Acting

In Focus on Acting we are going to look at the process of Acting as having three main components.

The first of these three components is that of **'Preparation'**; being all that takes place prior to 'on-camera' or 'live' performance. Preparation is a multi faceted area, with the actor having to utilize numerous resources available to bring their character to a state of readiness.

In this System we will look at possible Physical, Cognitive and Emotional preparations needed for character interaction. Different ways of achieving these preparation states will also be explored.

The second main area is the **'Interaction'**. 'Interaction' is simply the moment of performance, the time on screen or stage when you are living in an imaginary situation, 'truthfully'.

For many years there has been a catch-phrase which has haunted the traps. "Acting is Re-acting." I believe that acting is much more than re-acting, it is the reaction to cues given **and** the action the character takes as a result of those cues. To say that acting is re-acting I believe pacifies the action to instinctive reflex, leaving out the essential element of choice and characterization.

In this foundation system we will discuss how people interact, the non-verbal cues we react to, and various levels and stages of interaction. We will also look at the historical environment which informs the choices we make and why we interact the way we do.

The third area is that of **'Recovery'**. Recovery is the process that happens *after* the performance. Recovery may also happen during the performance however we shall deal with that situation when looking at Interaction.

Swimmers, Dancers, Athletes and many other professionals all need a process of recovery after their 'performance'. Swimmers may swim a few warm down laps, Dancers and Athletes may stretch after their exertions, the lawyer may go home for a scotch on the rocks while the Counsellor may need to vent with a colleague after becoming too attached in a particularly emotional case.

While the actor may be able to draw forth 'true' emotions for use in performance, it is very important that once the performance or scene is over they can recover from their state and quickly get on with preparation for the next scene.

Recovery is also very important to allow the actor the freedom to choose not to take the character home. In this method we will look at the important role of recovery, its place in 'risk taking', its place in 'Interaction' and its place in the overall psyche of the actor.

The actor who knows they can recover will take the greater risks necessary for some of the best performances.

## What makes up a Production?

In the entertainment industry, people are always talking about two main things when discussing film, theatre and television.

### 1) The Story

### 2) The Characters

Film, Theatre and Television projects can generally be viewed as driven primarily by one of these two things. Either they are mainly story driven;

**What happens is most important.**

Or Character driven;

**Who it happens to, is most important.**

## The Story

It is a very important role of the actor to make certain that the story is told. This is especially true of live theatre where the actors dictate the story and not the editor. While the scriptwriter obviously is the main source for story line and plot, how the director interprets the script and the behaviour of the 'characters' will also greatly effect the story that is eventually told.

See a play one night and the next night you may see a slightly different story being told, all depending on the particular circumstances unique to that performance. Ultimately it lies with the playwright to create the literary story, the director to define the story as they see it in performance and for the actors to tell that story to the audience.

Ideally the story told is a combination of the writer, director and actors, all contributing to the final product. In the case of film, you can add editor to that list. In film the editor and director have the most influence on the story told. Having said that, the buck stops with the Producer and so, for better or worse, they usually want to have their two cents, sorry, forty million dollars worth!

When telling the story, at various times we may want to stimulate the audience in specific ways. The three main ways are;

1) **Emotionally**

2) **Intellectually**

3) **Spiritually**

For the moment I'm not going to go into detail on these three ways of effecting the audience, that will come in a later Chapter. For now we just need to recognize that, some productions make you feel, some make you think and some inspire you! The way you portray your character and the method of presenting the audience with the plot will greatly effect the audience's experience.

While telling the 'story' well is an important role for the actor, more importantly is sharing the 'experience'. I believe this to be true for all creative influences on the performance. I have heard numerous times directors, producers etc stating to actors "Just tell the story". I believe this does our medium a great disservice. If you want to tell a 'story', write a novel, if you want to share an 'experience', put on a performance. I have seen many films & plays ruined by just-tell-the-story mentality. A theatrical experience is much, much more. The sights, sounds, musical score and moments of character development while not always adding to the story can greatly enhance the experience of the audience giving them a deeper & richer understanding. When I watched the Cinema release of Lord of the Rings directed by Peter Jackson, I was told a good story. When I watched the extended version release, Peter Jackson shared an experience. I believe a lot of the heart was cut out of the films for the cinema, the editor I assume was told, "Just tell the story". The heart was put back in when the extended version was released. So please, avoid where possible merely telling a story, instead share an experience with your audience. Now let's have a quick look at 'Character'.

**The Characters**

What are characters? Who are these people that we are trying to portray? If these characters are unique 'selves' how do we define self? What makes us up? To understand and bring truthfully to life a character we must first look at what it is that separates us into unique individuals.

What makes people different from one another? Sure we all look different in our own way but what truly defines us as unique? If we are to try to create a character with a truth and honesty to them, then it is important that we understand exactly what it is that makes a character special.

## *Choices*

Perhaps the main thing that differentiates us into individuals, or characters, is the choices we make. How individual would we be if we all made the same choices? If every-one chose the same thing on a menu, if every-one wanted to do the same career, if everyone wanted the same car? How unique would we be!?

What types of choices do we make? Generally speaking the choices we make fall into one of the following categories. These categories provide the defining components of 'self'.

1) **Intellectual Choice**

Eg, Should I drive the main road or take the shortcut?

2) **Emotional Choice**

Eg, Do I feel hurt because she teased me or will I feel angry?

3) **Physical Choice**

Eg, Would now be a good time to take my hand out of the fire?

4) **Spiritual Choice**

Eg, Do I let love guide me or fear?

The choices that we make now have their roots in

the past. Characters are defined by their actions and their actions are schooled by their personal background. We will look at character histories later; the events in these histories create the stepping-stones for current behavioral patterns.

Many of the choices that we make are so tied up in the past that they are now 'automatic'. The choices made when young can define the barriers of today. You probably don't break down into tears when someone sits in your favorite seat, however, when you were two or three years old you may very well have done.

As a child you were conditioned, told that crying in that situation was not appropriate, upon seeing that it was beneficial not to cry, ie, you received positive re-enforcement from a parent, you gradually made the choice not to cry.

Where did our choices begin? Where did we form, and how did we form the basis by which our individual decisions would be made?

As a child coming into a world we knew nothing about, we searched our environment for answers. We soon found them. We soon learnt that when we cried, mum or dad would come with food or to change our nappy. We quickly caught on that if we cried, we would get attention irrespective of whether or not we were hungry or things were getting uncomfortable down below. If we then quieten down we get even more attention in hugs from mum and dad, and so the basic foundations for future learning are acquired from these intrinsic needs.

I do not suggest that learning is as simple a process as I have, and will, illustrate however you are studying to be an actor and not a psychologist and so for now simplicity will serve you best.

## *Choices and Decision Making*

Herman, our illustrious three year old, wants attention from his mother and the way in which he goes about getting it will be a result of what has worked in the past for him.

Herman, as a baby, learnt that crying would result in attention and so now he tries opening the floodgates and letting the tears flow. Unfortunately Herman's crying, in this case, leads nowhere, his mother is ignoring him.

Herman decides that going up and grabbing his mothers dress and pulling it should do the trick. Alas, Herman's mother goes on talking to her neighbor and so has failed. Well if first you don't succeed try again. This time Herman chooses the screaming approach; he thinks that's sure to work! But his mother is a tough one and so continues to ignore him. Finally Herman decides to pull out his trump card and so leaves his mother and smashes a vase. Bingo! Mum comes over and belts him.

Herman achieved the attention he was after, his choice of action, breaking the vase, was reinforced.

'Operant' Conditioning is a behaviouristic learning theory where the result of a behavior reinforces the behavior/s that precedes it. In the previous example of Herman's behavior - smashing the vase, resulted in attention, a favorable outcome, thus the act of smashing the vase was reinforced and so he is more likely to make that decision or one similar, in the future.

## *Other*

This is one of the ways in which we learn. We learn and act as a result of the 'Other'. The idea of learning as a result of the other person, or **'Other'**, is a very important one and it will be referred to numerous times throughout this book.

**'Other'** refers simply to, **'something else'**. It is often another person or people, but it can also be an environment, an object or item, a thought, a sensation/stimulus, basically anything that becomes salient (Obvious) in the moment and is not a part of current perception. An 'Other' can also encompass a group of objects or people forming an 'Other' **'Chunk'**. A chunk is simply the term we will use to refer to a group of 'Others' that merge together in perception to form an individual chunk.

For example we may watch a flock of birds as a 'Chunk', a bowl of marbles, a soccer team running onto the field or a group at a party. We may also watch a 'chunk' of marathon runners and then focus in on individuals, just as we may look at a beach or study a grain of sand.

'Other' will be expanded upon extensively throughout this book.

Okay great, Herman has learnt some behavior. What about emotion? Does emotion work the same way? Lets have a look at Herman as a one year old. Our hero has just fallen out of his bunk, normally to get attention he would cry and in would come the cavalry. However this time mum is present, he already has her attention. Herman is left with the task of working out what to do. What does he do? He searches his environment for the answer. He looks straight at mum, eyes wide, holding his breath, waiting, watching, after all she's mum she should know what to do. Now it's up to the heroine to decide Herman's fate, does he laugh, cry, sing, dance or what?

If mum has a pained expression on her face and a look of fear or great concern then Herman sees that, recognizes that something is terribly wrong and bursts into tears. Mum comes over and hugs him, his crying in that situation is reinforced and so he learns.

If mum had smiled and looked as though everything was alright, as long as Herman wasn't too badly hurt, he would probably start to giggle or smile. Mum would give him a hug and so he would learn.

In the first case Herman learnt that if he gets hurt crying will bring about more attention. In the second example he learnt that smiling or laughing will give him attention. In the future Herman is more likely to adopt the behavior that has had the most favorable outcome in previous experiences.

Ok, so maybe it works for kids, but what about teenagers or adults? Let's look at Herman at the age of fourteen when his parents, the happy loving couple that they are, leave him alone at home for the first time.

Herman, being the perfect teenager that he is, goes to bed early. While lying in bed he hears a noise in the house. Immediately his heart starts beating faster and other physiological arousals take place.

Herman doesn't know what to feel yet because he still doesn't know what caused the noise. Unfortunately Herman has a vivid imagination and since he just finished watching a horror movie, fear sets in quickly.

Even though fear is dominating his emotions at this time he still doesn't know what the noise was and so he is reacting to his internal environment, his imagination.

Now Herman goes looking for the answer in his external environment. He still hasn't firmly 'labeled', or chosen, his appropriate emotion. Being a brave young lad, Herman starts walking through the house to see what caused the noise.

Let's now have a look at two hypothetical situational outcomes.

The first sees Herman round a corner to discover that the cat has knocked over a pot-plant. Herman now has the chance to 'label' his emotion with an external cue. Herman is overcome by relief, breaths out heavily, laughs to himself and goes back to bed. His behavioral choice and subsequent emotion has been a result of the 'Other'; ie, a result of the cat being the culprit and not some killer that he had dreamed up in his imagination. His effective emotion or his feeling of relief has replaced his initial emotion of fear. Herman feels relief because of the cat, the 'other'.

Now let's look at the second possible outcome, remembering that as Herman rounds the corner his internal state is identical in both examples. This time when Herman rounds the corner he faces a large bearded man - Boris, carrying two raised bloody knives. Herman now has the chance to 'label' his physiological arousal with an emotion stemming from an external cue. Herman is gripped with fear and so runs. He runs because of Boris, the 'other'.

Herman didn't choose to feel fear it was merely a reaction to his environment, although he did choose, consciously or unconsciously, to keep it.

We are not only interested in reaction but also interaction and so we look at the choices that Herman did make, ie, to run and to keep fear as his 'effective' emotion. Herman's choice to run and the maintenance of his emotion, fear, are aspects of his character.

If for example Tony, our black belt martial artist, was in the same given circumstances as Herman, his initial emotion would also have been labeled fear. However, unlike Herman, Tony chooses not to continue with this fear and instead turns it into aggression and rage and so attacks the unsuspecting Boris.

At some stage in the interaction (which we will look at in the next Chapter) Tony has made the decision to see this stimulus as a cue for anger as opposed to fear.

**TONY**

Tony's *'Initial'* emotion was **fear**
Tony's *'effective'* emotion was **anger**.

**HERMAN**

Herman's *'Initial'* emotion was **fear**.
Herman's *'effective'* emotion was **fear**.

Both stemming from the same stimulus, both illustrating a different character trait/choice.

If you take this situation from another angle and look at it from Boris's point of view, we find the same thing happening in him.

When Herman rounded the corner Boris's emotion may have been of dominance. Boris closely watches Herman for his reaction, Herman runs and so Boris's dominating feeling is reinforced, he wants to cause fear, and so pursues. Boris 'chases' because 'Herman runs', because of the 'Other'.

Now when Tony rounds the corner Boris still has the initial dominating feeling and waits for Tony's reaction. In this case Tony turns his fear to anger and aggression and so now Boris's initial emotion of dominance is changed by his environment into another emotion, fear, anxiety, defensive, vulnerable or what ever makes Boris tick, depending on his character.

Let's say Boris is really a big wimp, he sees Tony advancing on him; his dominance turns to fear and so he runs away screaming. His reaction is because of Tony, the 'Other'.

Experience is what gives us choices about the emotions we change; ie, Tony changing his fear to aggression is a result of what has worked for him in the past. Running away has worked for Herman and so that was his action.

*****

**All the choices made, behavioural, intellectual and emotional, were a result of the 'Other'. As actors one of the most fundamental hurdles you must jump is to get the focus off yourself and onto the 'Other'!!**

*****

Who your character is will be determined by their reactions and actions as a result of the 'Other'. 'Other' will be looked at throughout this book; it is one of the foundation stones of the 'Carne Method'.

To secure a solid foundation you need to understand and come to terms with your own initial natural reactions. The 'truthful' emotion, or the most basic emotion that has been elicited by the situation, is an emotion that will be common amongst nearly all people in a given culture. In the previous example practically every-one from our society would initially feel fear. However, our own unique *character* may change that emotion and dictate the behavioral response.

This 'universality' of the 'Primary' or 'Initial' emotion is a point in the interaction where actors can truthfully tap into another characters feelings and so portray them in an honest way. When you know how you feel in any given situation, on a basic, truthful, primary level, you can then put the choice of a character on top and so bring it to life.

## *How do we go about changing an Initial emotion?*

Firstly we know that the initial feeling or emotion is going to be cued in either the internal or external environment. For the moment we shall look at the external environment.

### *Perception*

The initial feeling or emotion we experience does not require any thought past a basic **'perception'**;

'Large man with raised bloody knives'- *fear*.

### *Primary Cognition*

It is after this initial perception that **'Primary Cognition'** occurs.

In 'Primary Cognition' the subject puts some very preliminary thoughts to his/her environment;

**Perception** – Large man with raised bloody knives – 'Fear'

**Primary Cognition** – 'I need to be safe'

I should point out that at this stage both Tony, our intrepid martial artist, and Herman have much the same cognitive pattern. The reason for this is that they haven't reached a sufficient level of cognitive functioning (thinking) to promote an active choice action. Tony, like Herman, associates 'Large man with raised bloody knives' with fear.

## Tertiary Cognition

The next level sees **'Tertiary Cognition'**. In Tertiary Cognition the subject processes the situation on a far deeper level. It is at this stage that Tony decides to fight back and Herman decides to stay with his initial emotion and run.

**Perception** – Large man with raised bloody knives – 'Fear'
**Primary Cognition** – 'I need to be safe.'
**Tertiary Cognition** – 'How am I going to be safe?'

**The stages with Perception & Primary Cognition are more or less the same for everyone in a given culture. It is in Tertiary Cognition where our unique choices are made.**

Herman, in Primary Cognition, needs to be safe and ends up running. Tony, in Primary Cognition, needs to be safe and ends up fighting. Herman's mother, in Primary Cognition, would also have needed to be safe and so possibly decided to scream for help. It isn't until Tertiary Cognition occurs that the individual evaluates a course of action, and in such, **defines their character.**

What you need to identify within yourself is your own Initial/Primary Emotion during Perception and Primary Cognition, and the choices you, as an individual, make after that. When you know this you can throw away your own 'labels' and put on a character's emotional labels.

You can take your own honest, truthful, **Initial Emotion** and then, while staying connected to the 'Other', re-label it to a characters' **Effective Emotion** giving a performance that has it's foundation in 'truth'.

Although the above example with Tony, Herman and Boris has been extreme it works to all levels of interaction as will be discussed in more detail in later Chapters.

Perception, Primary Cognition, Tertiary Cognition and 'labels' will all be dealt with in the next Chapter in greater depth.

### What are we up against?

To find out what we initially feel is not as easy as it sounds. We are so used to putting up defenses and barricades to protect us from the big bad world that we learn to very quickly 'put on' certain labels in certain situations and thus this re-labeling becomes a part of our character. We pre-program behaviors throughout life in order to deal more efficiently and effectively in our social world.

Sociologically, in our culture, crying is not generally regarded as a favorable male trait, and so the fear or hurt that is the Initial Emotion is suppressed and a more socially acceptable emotion becomes effective, ie, bravery, dominance, anger. It is not an easy job dissecting our individuality and peeling back the layers of barriers.

Firstly to get back to our Initial Emotions we need to focus on the environment, for that is where our emotions originate. How does this situation honestly make me feel?

Secondly, by taking away the capacity for decision, (the intellectual capacity to re-label the Initial Emotion in Tertiary Cognition), we allow for the feeling of this primary emotion to be experienced. In a later Chapter we will look at exercises designed to let you hook in to your Initial Emotions. (See also Appendix A)

## So how does it work?

We only have a certain amount of working room within our minds to think and evaluate. For example have you ever tried to study, read or work out a difficult problem with the T.V. going loudly and kids screaming wildly? It is much easier when all is quiet, without any disruptions.

In the above example the T.V. demands some attention, as do the kids. This means that your attention is divided between the T.V., kids and your task. Those distractions are forcing their way into your mind, taking up valuable cognitive resources.

In learning to re-discover your Initial Emotions you need to give your full attention to one thing and simply react to it. What do you honestly feel?

Try looking at someone in the eyes and working out a difficult mathematics problem without looking away or 'glazing' over. (ie, not focusing on them) It is extremely hard to do because the face in front of you demands attention and so your evaluative capability is diminished due to the dividing of your attention.

Inevitably you look away at the floor or wall, which doesn't demand as much attention, mental resources or barriers of protection, as a face. You free up cognitive space (head room) and so your capacity to work out the problem is increased. The same thing happens with emotion.

When looking someone in the face you will find it easier to respond in an initial way, if you don't take your eyes off them, keep breathing steadily and honestly 'connect' with them, ie, not looking 'through' them but truly being 'with' them.

Once your eyes move away, even slightly, your capacity to think is greatly increased and so you immediately go into Tertiary Cognition, decision, and away from your Initial Emotion. Also, when looking away, your body weight shifts off-center that also facilitates cognitive evaluation.

The notions of Primary and Tertiary thought, as well as the relative distribution of body weight, will be examined and further explained in the next Chapter.

Breathing is another very important factor when viewing the environment for emotional cues. As will be seen in the next Chapter, depending on which stage of Interaction you are in will effect where your breathing focus lies; on the 'in' or 'out' breath. When watching the other person you must keep breathing and not hold your breath. The 'in' breath allows the environment to effect you and with the 'out' breath, recovery and consolidation.

If you stop breathing, you stop being effected by the environment and disallow yourself any recovery. As you are neither 'here nor there' the body, emotion, mind and creativity all tense up and so, from an acting perspective, you die!

Breathing, and the associated stages, will be discussed further in Chapter 2.

## Tips for Learning in the Classroom

As I have mentioned this book is designed to give you a solid foundation on which to build your own, unique acting style. It is important for you to take classes from professional acting coaches at some point, in order to gain the practical experience necessary to hone your skills. I have put together some Tips and advice for when you are in the classroom.

1) Keep an honest and open relationship with your coach. Tell them what works for you and what doesn't. If something particularly traumatic has happened in your life recently, you don't need to tell them specifics but you should let them know that something has happened, as it will have an effect on your work. If your coach tells you to leave your personal life outside the classroom, ask them how? How do I allow my marriage break-up, P.M.T and the death of my mother not to effect me in class? This is a fair question. You will find times when you are working professionally and there are traumas in your personal life. How do you deal with them in regards to your performance? Open, honest relationship. Acting and acting tuition, is dealing with humans, real people and if your coach isn't sensitive to you as a real person then I suggest you find one who is.

2) Commit yourself fully to the exercises presented. Don't cop out! You will never learn as a result of merely attending a class. You must make the decision to be fully in the lesson, participate and actively process the information and exercises you explore. It is not enough to have a good teacher; you must be a good heuristic learner.

3) Be prepared to fail. Listen to me closely all you perfectionists out there. **BE PREPARED TO FAIL!** For some reason every student wants to be the best, and perfect, first time, every-time. **STOP IT!!** Scientists learned a long time ago the principle of trial and error. Use it!

During the class if you are focusing on being the best rather than learning then you are missing out BIG TIME! Drop the ego; there are enough in this industry already.

Take a risk with something you are not comfortable with, go out on a limb to learn. Maybe you aren't very good at playing angry characters, the next improvisation that you do, play a character who is angry. Perhaps you have a barrier with physical closeness, try kissing someone in a scene.

**Side Note:** Always use discretion when kissing or having intimate contact during an improvisation. I would only go through with the kiss if the other person were accepting. In the class you will get a 'feel' for what is acceptable with who, if you are unsure, ask. If you are playing a young couple madly in love, then obviously physical contact may play a big part in the scene, check first with the other actor! They may not yet be ready to go to a kiss etc in an improvisation, let them develop at their own pace. An actor needs to be virtually barrier free. Comes with the territory.

Talk with your coach and they will help you out. Constantly push yourself to be better in every situation. It doesn't matter if the scene you are doing in class is appallingly bad with people whispering behind their hands, "How bad is she!" "I can't believe they let her into this class!" Drop the ego you are there to learn. Be terrible, be bad ... better to do your bad stuff in the classroom than in the audition room. Take charge of your career, if you're not pushing your weaknesses (future strengths), or consolidating an idea, then what are you doing?

**Without failure there is no perfection!**

**Every 'failure' is actually a success in disguise.**

Keep trying new things; don't be put off by others. Take a professional approach and learn, and don't give up, after all, imagine what a world we'd live in if every scientist who tried to find a cure for cancer gave up if they failed on the first, second or even third attempt!

4) Be encouraging of others in the class. Again don't let your own ego rule. By helping them, you help yourself. Go out of your way to take aside that person who has been struggling and congratulate them for their determination and strength. Don't be afraid to ask others for help or comments on your work; push the ego aside and focus on learning. Be very objective with any comments you receive, while they 'may' be more experienced than you, it doesn't make them right. Use what works for you and ditch the rest.

5) Turn your mobile phone off! Not on silent, turn it off. The only exceptions are if you are expecting an urgent call, and I mean URGENT, in this situation you would check with your teacher that it's ok to leave it on. If they say no, then you would not participate in the class because the call is so urgent that you would forfeit your lesson for the call. The other reason would be for Emergency workers who are on call, again please check with your teacher first.

6) Questions, questions, questions. Ask lots and lots of questions. If you don't know something, then ask. Never be afraid to ask, even if it's simply to clarify a word that you don't understand. You have a right to learn, make the most of it.

**The only stupid question is the one not asked!**

## *Practical Exercises*

Take a moment right now to see how you are feeling. What emotions are present? Are you tense in any areas?

What I want you to start doing is become aware of how you are feeling at various times through the day.

Imagine that you have a little 'actor self' sitting on your shoulder watching what you are doing, how you are feeling, how you are reacting. Don't let the little 'actor' effect what you are doing or how you are doing it, just allow them to watch and absorb. Become consciously aware of yourself while in the motion of living.

These feelings and 'states' that you experience throughout the day are real and are an excellent source of inspiration for your work. The effortless efficiency that you go about day-to-day living needs to be present in your acting. Notice how you feel when taking a shower, you need that level of relaxation in front of a few dozen people and a camera ... while taking a shower. Your acting needs to become effortless.

So, the first thing I want you to do is go out and watch yourself living, making mental notes of how you are feeling and behaving while doing it. If you like, start a diary to relate various experiences.

The second thing I want you to do is to start watching other people. What are they doing? How are they reacting? How are they feeling? Also, and very importantly, watch them reacting off the 'Other'. Watch them looking at people and adjusting their behavior accordingly. Watch them interacting with their environment, watch them stub their toe and abuse a rock, watch them getting progressively frustrated and possibly angry as their anticipated 'Other' (the bus) does not turn up on time.

Start smiling at people and look them in the eyes, watch as they react to you. Their behavior is because of you, their 'other'.

Hopefully you are starting to realize how important it is to stay connected to the 'other' as an actor. Your actual performance originates there, not in you.

Thirdly go and watch films and plays. Is the story **Character** driven, **Story** driven or a nice mix of both? Do I care about the characters? Is the production trying to stimulate me emotionally, intellectually, spiritually, or a mix?

A little side note – It is very important that the audience cares about the characters, they may care that the hero lives or may really want to see the baddie go down, either way it is important that the audience cares about them. 'Caring' about characters will be looked at again later in this book. While watching films see the difference between characters you care about, Love or Hate, and those you don't.

While watching movies I want you to be consciously aware of not holding your breath. Whether the film is action, drama, horror or comedy, breathe continuously. This is a very important exercise. Often in scary movies or during moments of high suspense we hold our breath. When this happens we cut off and push down our initial emotion, which during horror or suspense will generally be – Fear. Make sure that you keep breathing as this will allow the film to more fully effect you and you will be better able to identify your initial emotion. Also make certain that you don't fold your arms or cross your legs. These barriers help you to 'deal' with, or get away from the emotion, I don't want you to 'deal' with it, I want you to feel it!

Make certain that you keep breathing during the sad scenes, again by breathing the emotion will be more fully experienced. Let the tears flow, don't hold back, don't stop the emotion let it have its full life, feel it, experience it, enjoy it! The same goes for all films, you'll suddenly find your body alive with feelings and it feels good! Again, this is an excellent exercise for getting in touch with your initial emotions.

If you get a chance, watch some young children (1 - 3yrs) playing. Their interactions are happening without the restraints of adult barriers. Their behavior and emotions displayed are generally from their 'Initial Emotion'. If they get hurt, they cry, if they want something, they take it. Watch how they learn and interact with their 'Others'.

Start to try and recognize your own initial and effective emotions. If you find yourself angry, try and work out what the Initial emotion behind it is; Are you actually hurt because they forgot your birthday? Are you really happy when telling your friends that your marriage is going great or are you covering? Try to be totally honest with yourself and look into those places that you'd probably rather not and see what actually makes you tick.

Try and identify any events in the past that may have had a big influence on the choices that you make today. Look into your own history and see if you can find some defining moments, moments that have shaped the way in which you deal with the world.

**Remember**

1) Take the focus off yourself and place it onto the **'Other'**. The 'Other' is the source of your creativity and inspiration.

2) Re-discover your own Initial/Primary Emotions, because it is in these emotions that you share commonality with other characters. Once you can identify your own **Initial/Primary** emotions you can re-label them within the **Tertiary Cognition** stage and thus bring another character to life using your own 'truth'.

3) Great Actors evolve their own way of working from a solid foundation.

Well I think that's about enough for now, that should keep you busy for a while. Don't become overwhelmed by everything, take your time, there is no rush, consistency is most important. A little a day and soon you'll be well on your way to being a great actor!

# CHAPTER 2

# *The Interaction*

## THE INTERACTION IN DETAIL

In the Carne Method we will break down human interaction into five stages and closely look at what happens during each of these stages. The reason we do this is so we can understand what is happening at each level of the Interaction and thus dissect it for character understanding and creation. Different characters often dwell in different stages of the interaction.

## Stages of Interaction

### Stage 1 – First Contact

'**First Contact**' is the initial stage of interaction and occurs before we even cognitively perceive what is happening.

### Cue

In 'First Contact' the **cue** is either external or internal. This is the stage when the initial physiological arousal occurs, as yet there is no emotion labeled onto it.

A point of interest is that psychological studies have supported the notion that all emotions have very similar physiological states, which is why the initial arousal can spring to any emotion that the 'Other', external or internal, dictates. (Don't worry too much about this now, it will become clearer in later Chapters)

### Intellectually

At an intellectual level very little is happening. As yet you don't know what the stimulus is, just that your senses have detected something 'Other' than what previously *was*.

## Emotionally

With the cue, or initial stimulus, comes the physiological arousal and an accompanying movement of body weight shifting up and away. As yet there is no salient emotion, just the base physiological arousal upon which the subsequent emotion will ride.

If you have ever had someone jump out from behind a doorway and scare you, you will appreciate the physiological arousal involved and the shift of body weight up & away from the source. This is an obvious and big example of the 'First Contact' stage. In the first moment you don't know yet what it is, nor what is happening, it is merely the initial stimulus. In the first stage it doesn't matter whether it's Boris with his knives or your sister that jumps out, the *initial* shock is the same. It isn't until the next stage, when perception occurs, that the difference is experienced.

The 'First Contact' stage is an 'uncertain' stage, as yet details are not known, consequently the focus is directed towards the cue (internal or external) to ascertain the situation.

The whole **feel** of the First Contact stage is 'up'. The **body weight goes up,** the **voice goes up,** and the **breath focus is in.**

## Vocally

As mentioned 'First Contact' is an 'uncertain' stage. You don't know what is happening, but your body does try to find out, by placing focus on the cue.

Vocally the voice is higher in your range, which is a characteristic of an uncertain stage. So, someone has jumped out in front of you in a dark alley at night and you scream. The scream is a sign that you are in the First Contact stage and haven't yet progressed to the next stage. Once perception occurs, the potential is there for you to move on.

When asking a question the inflection will be up. The raise in pitch is an indicator of an uncertain stage, unknowing; ie, you want to know something.

Try right now saying the following line out loud as a question.

"I love you?"

Now try saying it as a statement.

"I love you."

The inflection is different in each case, the first inflection was up - **'Uncertain Stage'**
The second inflection was down - **'Knowing Stage'**
Some characters may have an upward inflection even when not asking a question, this could signify an uncertainty in their character, or simply reflect someones ongoing, outward focus in order to maintain the 'others' attention.

## Physically

Physically there is an upward movement in body weight. There is also a slight movement away from the stimulus, giving you room to identify what the stimulus is. Sometimes it's a big movement and at other times it is barely noticeable. Someone calls your name, you turn, eyebrows slightly raised. Someone jumps out at you and you leap (well maybe not leap) into the air.

Physiologically your body prepares for action. Heart starts beating faster, pumping blood around your body. Pupils dilate, adrenalin is produced etc. This physiological arousal is going to provide the base for the emotion that your intellect will soon label.

It is important to note how everything ties in, the body, emotion, voice, breath etc. If you have ever seen someone in 'shock' you may have noticed that their eyes are wide, eyebrows up, voice higher and carrying themselves in a very `up' way. As yet they haven't progressed through to the next stage and so are stuck in 'First Contact'.

If a surprise in 'First Contact' occurs in a physical way, ie, you are grabbed from behind, then the events are exactly the same, except that it is a result of a physical stimulus rather than visual. Auditory, olfaction, touch, visual or taste sensations all have the same series of events follow.

For example if you taste something nice that you didn't expect to be, eyebrows go up, a mmmmm sound with an upward inflection occurs.

The same applies for your sense of smell. Smell a flower that surprises you with a pleasant scent and the inflection is up. The feeling is like, "I didn't realize this would smell so nice".

A loud noise behind you may make you jump and possibly scream. Again, this is a reaction to an as yet unknown stimulus.

This first stage, 'First Contact', is very important in that this is the instance when new information is received. The actor must not anticipate the next action, dialogue, motive... etc in a scene as this will make the 'surprise' of new information/stimulus false. The actor must master this stage to have their reaction truthful and natural. The way we achieve this, as I will talk about later in more depth, is to stay 'connected' to the 'Other'. In most cases the other person. The other person, generally, is where your surprise will originate, if you are not connected with the other actor/s then the surprise will be a fabrication of yourself and not a true reaction.

This 'connectedness' to the 'Other', can be achieved through any of the senses.

The surprise in 'First Contact' does not have to be big. In fact, more than 95% of the time First Contact is very subtle. For example, if someone calls out your name, the upward shift may take place only in the eyebrows. At the sound of your name you may turn around, eyebrows up, to see who it is. 'First Contact' can be even more subtle. With all new information comes a surprise, and with it, an upward shift. A great deal of the time the shift is so subtle that it is, for the most part, undetectable. However, the shift at some level does occur.

To proceed through the 'First Contact' stage you must first realize **and** accept what has happened. In the example with Herman and Boris, let's say that Herman goes into a state of shock when seeing Boris. Herman becomes 'stuck' in the 'First Contact' stage. Body weight up, breath focus in etc... The most likely reason he has become stuck in this stage is that, while he has realized that there is this large bearded man in front of him holding raised bloody knives, he has not yet accepted it.

A young child, who has witnessed some horrible occurrence, may realize, but not accept, the situation. Their voice would be up and their whole body carried with an upward energy. Once they realize **and** accept what has happened, the body weight comes down and is centered, the voice lowers and the breath focus is out.

People who have had a particularly traumatic experience may go into shock as their mind refuses to accept what has happened. We have all had an extended 'First Contact' stage before. Maybe it was on the news of a death;

"No, no, it isn't true. No. I was only speaking to them yesterday"

Maybe an excellent result in an exam;

"I can't believe it, wow! Oh my god! They must have made a mistake!"

Or any of the infinite other situations we may find our selves in where our mind initially can't accept the reality. However once you have realized and accepted the stimulus, you go into the next stage.

'First Contact' is an open exertion, a stage where new information is first taken on. The actor must be prepared to take a 'risk' with this stage. The risk is to not know what is going to happen next, and honestly 'live' in the situation. After this initial First Contact there comes a recovery with the perception. This recovery takes us into the second stage of the interaction model,

**'Realization/Acceptance.'**

### Stage 2 - 'Realization/Acceptance

The 'Realization/Acceptance' stage is cued from an internal source. The environment or the sensation that has formed the cue in the 'First Contact' stage is now likened to past experience.

### Intellectually

At an intellectual level the incoming information is processed via an initial **Perception.**

Perception is the most basic cognitive process; it is a simple label of recognition. It is as simple as;

> `Man with raised knives'
> `Cat'
> `Pain'
> 'nice smell'
> 'I've been grabbed'
> etc...

Remember it is these simple concepts that are realized and accepted.

Psychologists would relate these simple perceptions to basic 'Pattern Recognition'. Pattern recognition is where you liken the stimulus to an existing cognitive pattern, a reference point from past experience. Do I have a similar picture in my mind from a previous experience to what I now perceive?

Even if you have never seen Boris and his knives before, his appearance holds a similar pattern to other danger cues you have experienced before, either personally in life or in magazines, stories, Television news, films etc... This recognition of danger will let you know that it is fear you are experiencing.

**Emotionally**

It is with Pattern Recognition that the physiological arousal from the 'First Contact' stage is labeled with an initial reactive emotion. **Perception** sees the physiological arousal labeled with a **Primary** or **Initial Emotion**; ie,

| Perception | Initial Emotion |
|---|---|
| Boris | Fear |
| Mum | Love |
| Grand Canyon | Awe |
| Being teased | Hurt |

Etc...

It is this initial emotion that you need to be able to recognize within yourself. When you know how you're feeling at a 'Primary' level, you can bring characters truthfully to life without your own 'labels' or barriers getting in the way.

It is this initial emotion that will **motivate** your character. For example; In the case of seeing Boris with his knives your initial emotion is **fear**. Fear then motivates your action. If you eventually start running or fighting back or screaming for help, these behaviors are motivated by fear. Just like taking lots of pictures of the Grand Canyon would be motivated by awe, or the hurt from being teased may motivate you to punch someone.

Realization/Acceptance is a **recovery stage**; the

initial surprise is recovered from in the acknowledgment of perception. In recovery, the breath focus is out.

**Vocally**

Realization/Acceptance is a **'knowing'** stage, unlike 'First Contact', which was uncertain. In 'Realization/Acceptance' we now know what the stimulus is. This 'knowing' is expressed vocally by a lowering in pitch and can be seen in statements. The inflection in a statement is down because you know what is happening. As was seen previously in the statement,

"I love you."
is very differently delivered to the question,
"I love you?"

In the case of taste if you eat something that tastes nice and you knew it would then the perception of - **"This does taste good"** would have a mmmmm with a downward inflection.

As a general note, (I will go into more depth in a later Chapter) if you want to play a very 'sure-of-yourself' character, then your vocal tonality will generally be low. If, however you want to play some-one who never really 'understands' or 'realizes' anything then your pitch will be higher, as in 'First Contact'.

**Physically**

A characteristic of this 'knowing' stage is that the body weight is down and centered. In the 'First Contact' stage the weight was away from the center, indicating uncertainty. Characters who carry themselves physically with their body weight down and centered are generally fairly certain of themselves. This physicality indicates a sureness of character, a confidence born from knowing.

Yoda, in the film 'The Empire Strikes Back', gives us an interesting example of body weight and status. When Luke Skywalker first finds Yoda, Yoda's physicality and vocal qualities are all 'up' and 'off-center'. He is seen by Luke Skywalker as a joke. Upon the Realization by Luke that this funny creature is actually Yoda, Jedi master, we see Yoda go into a high status, confident, controlled character. His body weights sinks, his ears lower, and his voice drops.

As the body weight sinks the 'breath focus' is out. This exhalation sees the affirmation of knowledge of the stimulus.

### Stage 3 - 'Need

Like the Realization/Acceptance stage, the 'Need' stage is internally cued. It is in this stage that our most basic needs are experienced.

### Intellectually

In our example, Herman, our illustrious hero rounds the corner to find Boris, the knife wielding killing machine. Herman has experienced 'First Contact', realizes and accepts what has happened, and it is now that he **'needs'**, or has been motivated to do something about his environment. Herman works on his dilemma to a slightly greater intellectual depth. Herman enters **Primary Cognition**.

| Realization | | Need |
|---|---|---|
| **Perception** | ⇒ | **Primary Cognition** |
| Man with knives | | "I need to be safe" |

Herman needs to be safe, or, Herman is motivated by his environment to seek safety. In the case of Herman, he has processed the information to the level of;

**"I need to be safe"**

Tony, the martial artist, has also processed the information to the level of;

**"I need to be safe"**

As has been mentioned, most people in a given society will process almost identically to this level of cognition. What they subsequently do with this cognitive processing shall be a character choice. The need embodies the **'Objective'** of the character. So if you need to be safe, then your objective is to be safe.

## *Emotionally*

In this stage the physiological arousal and subsequent emotion is reinforced.

When Herman 'realized' what was happening, his physiological arousal was labeled with an emotion. Now Herman needs to act on this emotion, the emotion and arousal are reinforced by this need.

Herman experienced fear in the Realization/Acceptance stage because of his perceived threat. On entering the Need stage Herman took the small intellectual step of;

| **Realization/Acceptance** | **Need** |
|---|---|
| I feel fear    ⇒ | I need to be safe. |

If Herman needs to be safe, then there must be some threat to his safety. This acknowledgement of 'I need to be safe' **reinforces** the initial fear. Still with me?

**Fear**
⇓
**I Need to be safe**
⇓
**Reinforced Fear.**

Ever been walking alone at night on a dark road

or path? For some reason you start to feel a bit scared. Maybe you heard something? Okay, so you're feeling a bit scared, you need to be safe, so you start walking a bit faster to get to your destination. Ever noticed how as you're walking faster your fear increases? Your body is sending back messages saying; *"Hey, I'm walking faster there must be something to be scared of!"*

Or, maybe you're home alone at night and you hear a noise in the house. You stop to listen; perhaps you hide under the sheets. As you perform these, 'I need to be safe' behaviors, you reinforce your fear and so it spirals. This doesn't only apply to fear but also other emotions.

The two main initial emotions are Fear and Love. Most **Effective Emotions**, the emotion you end up displaying, can be traced back to one of these two. The two main off chutes of these emotions are Hurt and Pride.

Eg, maybe you're **angry** because some-one has shouted at you, calling you a name. If we take that back one emotional step we find that the anger has come from **hurt**, you were hurt by what they called you. Go back one more step and we may find **fear**, a fear of not being **loved**. Generally all effective emotions can be traced back to love, or the fear of the absence of love.

Another example; Maybe you're feeling **happy** because a particular guy you like has asked you out on a date. Take this back one emotional step and we may find **pride**, you're proud that this person has affections for you. Take this back one more step and we find **love**. Unconditional acceptance for who you are.

## Physically

In this stage the body weight is up and centered. With the body weight up, Herman is allowing the environment to effect him and is now acting on it. We also observe that his weight is centered which, unlike in the surprise stage and away from center, shows a certainty or knowledge of what he is doing, ie, in Herman's case with Boris;

"I know I need to be safe".

In the Realization/Acceptance stage the body weight was also centered and also showed a 'knowledge' of the situation. However, unlike that stage, in Need the weight focus is upward.

In Realization/Acceptance the focus was inward, ie, Herman had to realize and accept, within himself, (likening to a Pattern Recognition) what was happening in the environment. Now, in the Need stage, his focus is again, like in `First Contact', outward on the environment. Herman needs to be safe and so looks to an 'Other' in which to seek refuge.

In this stage the breath focus is *in* which also gives an *outward* focus, almost as if breathing in the environment. In the case of Herman, he takes a deep breath and ends up running. If you have ever felt a real need to do something then you may have taken a deep breath and said'

**"Here goes nothing!"**

This is a heightened breath for a big outward focus. This happens again in the final stage, which shall be talked about soon.

The Need stage is a very important one for you to recognize within yourself. This is the stage immediately preceding character choices. If you can isolate this stage in yourself, then you can bring a role to life through yourself to this point, and then the `character' from here on. This allows the character to come from a `truthful' emotional state and thus gives an honest, truthful, emotive and hopefully inspiring performance. It should be apparent that this is a stage of exertion and as such has an outward focus, as can also be seen in the breath and body weight.

The next stage sees character choices and individuality come to life, the `**Evaluation Stage**'.

### Stage 4 – 'Evaluation'

Like the previous two stages, the Evaluation Stage is internally cued, with an external awareness. It is in this stage that you search for answers to your basic needs and formulate a plan of attack. This is also the stage when our individual human barriers and defenses come up.

**Intellectually**

In the 'Evaluation' stage you proceed past the basic need and into Tertiary Cognition, which sees the information processed at a much deeper level. Ie;

**'What am I going to do about it'?**

Tertiary cognition is the deeper processing of the situation at hand. One of the keys to Characterization is held in **Tertiary Cognition** for it is in the Evaluation Stage that the character's choices are made.

Again, in our example, Herman, our illustrious hero rounds the corner to find Boris, the knife wielding killing machine. Herman has experienced 'First Contact', Realizes and Accepts what has happened, has a basic Need as a result of his 'Other', it is now that he must decide what to do. Herman works on his dilemma to a much greater intellectual depth. Herman enters **Tertiary Cognition**.

### Realization/Acceptance
### Perception

Man with knives

(Fear)

⇓

### Need
### Primary Cognition

"I need to be safe"

(Reinforced Fear)

⇓

### Evaluation
### Tertiary Cognition

"How am I going to be safe?"

(What emotional barrier will I use?)

Herman now goes about trying to evaluate how he is going to be safe. This is the stage of 'internal conflict'. Does Herman run, fight back, scream for help, hug him, collapse...? How am I going to reach my objective?

**Herman's decision is a defining moment for his 'character'.**

All characters that you play will be defined by their actions, the decisions they make. Every time you make a decision you are defining a quality of your character.

Up until this point we have merely reacted to our 'Other'. It is now we make our own individual choice. **This is the moment that you can re-define your own 'truth'** (Initial Emotion & Need) **with a character's unique choice.** In this way you can bring your own truthful emotional state into the 'truth' of a character that you portray.

### First Contact
**Stimulus**
Physiological Arousal
⇓
### Realization/Acceptance
**Perception**
Man with knives
(**Fear**)
⇓
### Need
**Primary Cognition**
"I need to be safe"
(**Reinforced Fear**)
⇓
### Evaluation
**Tertiary Cognition**
"How am I going to be safe?"
(**Keep Fear?**)

⇓                ⇓

| **You The Actor** | **You The Character** |
|---|---|
| Run Away | Fire Machine Gun |
| (**Fear**) | (**Anger**) |

You go through the first three stages as yourself, ensuring a truthful base for your performance, and then in the Evaluation Stage re-define yourself as the character you are portraying.

*Emotionally*

It is in this stage of Evaluation that the initial emotion is questioned and thus the emotion possibly changed. Is this fear I'm feeling? Is this anger? The choice, conscious or unconscious, decides the eventual emotion expressed. Re-Labeling an Initial Emotion with an Effective Emotion provides the foundation of the Adult barriers that we carry around with us. People who are well guarded, or have very strong barriers would have a strong history of re-labeling initial emotions. They have buried their Primary Emotions under a sea of social barriers, behind a wall of re-labeled emotions.

Let's now have a look at some hypothetical emotional re-labeling occurring during the 'Evaluation' stage. Using Herman's situation, Tony, a legendary martial artist confronts Boris and;

### First Contact
**Stimulus**
Physiological Arousal
⇓

### Realization/Acceptance
**Perception**
Man with knives
(Fear)
⇓

### Need
**Primary Cognition**
"I need to be safe"
(Reinforced Fear)
⇓

### Evaluation
**Tertiary Cognition**
"How am I going to be safe?"

Now Tony evaluates the best means to achieve his safety. It is now that Tony decides, unconsciously, to turn his initial fear into rage or aggression and fight Boris. Herman, on the other hand, decides in this stage of evaluation to stay with his initial feelings of fear and run. It is in this stage that Herman's mother would decide to scream for help. All these choices are a result of the person's background, upbringing and current given circumstances.

If Herman found that when he was a child running got him out of trouble most efficiently, then this is most likely what he will adopt. Tony doesn't necessarily have to change his fear to rage in order to fight, he merely judges fighting as his best behavioral option given his particular history.

**Another Example**

Rhonda, our sixteen-year-old neurotic schoolgirl, is confronted with Herman, our seventeen year old 'stud', at a party. Herman has had his eye on Rhonda for a while now and this is his chance to make a move. Rhonda has admired Herman from afar but decided that he could never fall in love, or even like a person as 'ugly' as herself. Herman moves in to say hello to Rhonda. Smiling, Herman walks up and says;

**"Hello"**

Rhonda, after her initial First Contact, realizes that Herman, the guy she likes, has said hello and is smiling at her. Rhonda immediately labels her emotion as love. Rhonda now has a need, or motivation, to express her feelings. Unfortunately, as has been mentioned, Rhonda is neurotic and is yet to go through the Evaluation Stage. Rhonda, on entering 'Tertiary Cognition', remembers that Herman could never possibly be interested, or attracted to her and so evaluates that she is being set up for some sort of joke. Now Rhonda re-labels her primary emotion, love, to one of hurt and so slaps Herman across the face. The secondary, or Effective Emotion, is expressed.

Tony, Rhonda's brother and legendary martial artist, sees what has happened from a distance. After Tony's initial 'surprise' he realizes that his sister has slapped someone across the face and so labels his physiological arousal $\Rightarrow$ concern.

Tony now has a need or motivation to investigate. Next we see Tony move into the Evaluation stage and start formulating a plan of attack. He thinks to himself that his sister would never slap anyone without good reason and so concludes that this other person must have either hurt her or insulted her in some way. Tony's Primary Emotion, concern, is now re-labeled with rage and so he rushes over to the scene intending to bestow bodily harm upon Herman.

Poor old Herman sees Rhonda's brother coming and assesses the situation quickly. Although a stud, Herman is not much of a fighter and his Primary Emotion, fear, is held onto solidly in the Evaluation stage and thus Herman flees in a great hurry wondering why he leads such a charmed life.

When Rhonda changed her emotion from love to hurt, her evaluation was made with 'hurt' becoming the Effective Emotion. As an actor if you can put another persons, or characters, 'label' on top of your own Primary Emotion, you can then evaluate the situation through that character in order to embody the role.

Emotions change very quickly in tune with the environment. This is only one reason that actors should be attentive and totally focused on what is happening at all times within a performance. Your Emotions originate from within your performance environment, cut yourself off from the environment, 'Other', and you cut off your source of creativity.

**Physically**

The body weight during this stage is off-center and shifting. As can be seen in the 'First Contact' stage, this `off centeredness' indicates an 'uncertainty' which is obvious given that the person is evaluating a situation. If a person is off center, or has a shifting of body weight, then they are in an evaluation state.

Often, when making a decision, we tilt our heads to the side while thinking. At times people waver their hand from side to side, or when confronted with a question to which they want to lie in their answer, they will shift from one foot to the other while deciding. This is usually very subtle. It's like a tugging of forces, this way or that way, an 'internal conflict'.

Some people pace around when thinking, this being a big shift of weight across a distance. If you regard someone, you may tilt your head to the side, as can also happen if you don't agree with someone but are thinking about what they have said. The famous Clint Eastwood Character, 'Dirty Harry', doesn't shift from side to side when silhouetted from behind because he is *so* confident, he knows he's going to win. No evaluation needed.

However 'Raymond', played by Dustin Hoffman in the film 'Rain Man', has a physicality which is continually shifting as his character is in an almost constant state of evaluation.

The shift in weight can be quite small, slight shift to the side, or large, pacing around a room. It is also a very clear indicator that an Initial Emotion is being, or has been, relabeled.

If you have ever spoken or done a performance in front of a live audience you may have been nervous. A sign of nerves is this shifting of weight, seen as a slight trembling or shaking somewhere in the body. What is happening is that your Initial Emotion is fear and during the evaluation stage you are trying like crazy to get rid of the fear and label it as something else. The shaking of your body is telling you that you are trying to get away from your Initial Emotion.

How do we get over those nerves and 'Stage Fright'? We'll look at that in greater depth during the final Chapters.

**The Breath**

In this stage the breath, like the body, is generally shifting with slightly more focus placed on the out breath as you try to 'Realize' a solution. In a state of high anxiety you may find yourself taking short, quick, shallow breaths as you grapple with trying to make a decision.

As mentioned, one sign that a Primary Emotion has been changed is a manifestation of this emotion somewhere in the body. For example, if your Primary Emotion was fear and your Effective Emotion, the one expressed, rage, then you might find your hands trembling or even a tightness in your throat. If you have ever strongly held back tears then you will appreciate the almost choking effect it can have on your throat as you try to hold back the strong initial emotion.

If your Primary Emotion is hurt and your Effective Emotion calm, then this usually manifests into twitching, ie, hands, feet and also a tightening in the throat. I've found that quite a few people hold the tension in their jaws.

Defending yourself from the world usually means a great deal of re-labeling, it would not look good if every time your boss told you to work harder you burst into tears. This constant re-labeling of emotions, as is apparent in stress, ends up holding up somewhere in the body. Different people take this physical manifestation into different parts of the body.

A 'high flying' executive, who is ruthless and shows very little emotion when making huge decisions, is usually re-labeling like crazy. This person often takes the physical manifestation of re-labeling into the neck and shoulders. As a result the tension and tightness in the shoulders is huge and so they often have massages, or work out in the office gym, to alleviate the built up stress. As they start to relax the emphasis is on the out breath which enhances the recovery.

It is important for you as an actor to become in touch with your body and realize where you take on stress. I believe to fulfill your potential as an actor you need to be in touch with your emotions. If you are in tune with your body you will be able to identify when you are re-labeling an Initial Emotion. This aspect of training will be dealt with in detail later.

Tertiary Cognition allows the person, or character, to assess the situation and to work out the best plan of attack. It is then that a decision is made about what to do. All that is now needed is for our subject to act upon the first four stages. This leads us to the fifth and final stage, **'Commitment'**.

### Stage 5 - *'Commitment'*

The **'Commitment'** stage is basically the response resultant from the initial First Contact.

*Intellectually*

In the Commitment stage your decision/choice has been made and is now being acted upon. 'Herman running' is in the 'Commitment Stage.' Your focus in this stage is out, connecting with the 'Other', and ready to **Perceive**, **Realize** and **Accept** the next **stimulus**.

*Emotionally*

In the Commitment stage the labeled physiological arousal, the emotion, has been decided and is now being acted upon. This Effective Emotion is now expressed.

As you may recall, Rhonda, our sixteen year old neurotic, changed her initial emotion, Love, to Hurt. It was through this Hurt that she decided to slap Herman across the face. Her slapping of Herman illustrated the 'Commitment' stage.

*Physically*

Physically the body weight is up and slightly forward. The focus in this stage is out and so the physicality expresses 'doing', 'going forward', making a 'commitment'.

## Interaction in Motion

The process of interaction, the time taken to complete and even the overlapping of many interactions within the one person is a very complex one. The time taken to go through an interaction can be as short as a fraction of a second, to a couple of minutes, to months or even years.

It is common for a person to start an interaction and not complete it. We shall firstly look at an interaction that takes a mere fraction of a second.

This example is one of the simplest interactions. Herman's mother wants to ask Herman a question and in the Evaluation stage she aptly works out that she must first get his attention. Herman's Mother, Marge, addresses Herman by simply using his name;

**"Herman"**

On hearing his name Herman quickly realizes that his name has been used, needs to find out why, evaluates that the tone his mother used did not infer trouble and so in the 'Commitment' stage answers;

**"Yes"**

This interaction would usually take less than a second to complete. You may notice that even in this short example there is every stage present. If Marge's voice implied that she was angry with Herman, the interaction may have taken a couple of seconds with Herman trying to work out what he had done wrong or how to get out of the pending trouble.

To illustrate an interaction of a couple of minutes we shall use our neurotic sixteen year old, Rhonda.

Rhonda has just gone into a dress shop and has spied a beautiful dress that she would love to buy. She finds out from the shop assistant that they have the dress in her size. Rhonda now goes to the dress on show and looks at the price tag. Rhonda gets a big surprise in 'First Contact'. After the initial surprise Rhonda realizes and accepts how expensive the garment is. Rhonda now moves into the Need stage. Rhonda reaches for her credit card. Before she gets to it, Rhonda enters the evaluation stage. Now our heroine is torn between buying the dress and the fact that she can't really afford it. Rhonda's thoughts go something like this;

"I have to buy this dress.
I haven't got enough money in the bank.
I've got a month to pay it off.
I won't be able to save enough money in that time.
If I don't go out I may be able to afford it.
I've got no will power, I couldn't stay home for a month.
Maybe mum will loan me the money.
No, I already owe her a hundred dollars.
What if I sold my bike and some Blue-Ray Discs.
No, I like my bike and only death will part me and my Blue-Ray's.
If I work over-time maybe I could get enough.
Things haven't been the best I doubt there'll be any more over time for a while.
Damn, it I'll buy it and work out how to pay for it later!"

Rhonda now goes into the Commitment Stage and buys the item.

Now let's have a look at an interaction that could take a couple of days. In the last example, the stage that took the longest to complete was the Evaluation Stage. In this next example the stage at which the recipient is 'stuck' is in 'First Contact'.

Marge, Herman's mother, has just died. Herman gets the initial shock. For Herman to enter the Realization/Acceptance Stage he must first realize and accept what has happened. Unfortunately Herman will not, or can not, accept that his mother is dead and so remains in the 'First Contact' Stage. No tears have come yet, the tears flow as a release, or recovery, which comes in the Realization/Acceptance stage.

Herman refuses to accept his mothers death. Herman races through the house looking for his mother. He rings up some of his mothers friends to find out if she's there. His energy is up, his body weight is up, he is in what most people would classify as, shock. For three days Herman's eyes are wide, voice higher than usual and carrying himself with an 'up' energy, often heard saying;

No, no..."

On the forth day he goes to his mother's funeral. On seeing her body being lowered into the grave Herman finally accepts what has happened and bursts into tears.

Herman now has a 'Need' to be comforted and to feel secure. On being consoled by some close friends, Herman now evaluates what has happened and has to make a decision about what he is going to do. After a few days in contemplation Herman decides that he must get on with his life. Still upset and not totally recovered Herman goes back to his usual routine.

Now we shall look at an interaction that may take a number of months.

Tony, Our martial arts hero, has enlisted in the army. Unfortunately, as is usually the case with my examples, war breaks out and Tony is sent to fight in the Middle East. Tony, while on a special mission involving penetration into enemy territory, steps on a land mine and has his right leg blown off.

Tony gets the 'First Contact' but, like the previous example, refuses to accept his loss and so goes into 'shock'. Tony refuses to accept his loss. Even on arrival home to Australia, Tony cannot believe that he has lost a leg. In this case it could take several months before Tony fully accepts the loss of his leg.

Some interactions take years to complete. Have you ever had an event happen to you that has plagued your mind intermittently over a number of years?

For example, when Herman was 14 a bully at school challenged him to a fight. There were a lot of people standing around watching when Herman pointed behind them to an imaginary teacher and yelled;

**"Teacher!"**

He then ran at high speed in the other direction. For months after Herman suffered for his display of 'cowardice'. For years later, every now and then, the incident would tear at Herman's emotions and he would briefly relive the feelings of the time.

As yet Herman still hasn't accepted his actions and wants to set them right. Herman would think;

**"If only I had ........ Instead of running away. "**

This is a type of interaction that may take years to finally finish, or may never be fully completed. Sound familiar in any way?

Some interactions may never actual be resolved. It is these interactions that can produce neuroses in a character, phobias, tensions, anxieties and even physical problems. For this illustration I shall give an example from my own life. Even though I have actually completed this interaction you will see how, if not for the right circumstances, it would have remained incomplete for my entire life. I believe most of us have some of these unresolved interactions that our conscious selves are totally unaware, but we are effected by them all the same. Some psychologists refer to this 'type' of thing as repressed memories, which is probably an accurate description.

When I was **three years old** I traveled around Australia with my parents. While traveling we stopped at a festival where my parents purchased a plastic spider for me. The spider was about the size of a men's wallet and had an elastic string that it bobbed up and down on.

When I was **twenty-one years old** I was talking with my parents about the trip, seeing how much of it I could remember. Something came up about this plastic spider I had owned. I remembered the spider vividly and tried to work out what had happened to it. I even went searching the house for it. I couldn't remember ever getting rid of it; I figured it must still be somewhere. No luck, no spider… Later on, still pondering the fate of this spider that I had now become very reattached to, I asked my mother if she knew what had happened to it. She told me that I was swinging it around my head near a campfire one night. At the time she told me not to swing it around as the elastic would break and it would end up in the fire. I had ignored her warning and sure enough the spider met its fate in the fire. As the story unfolded I found the memories come flooding back, the emotions included. When she mentioned that the spider had gone into the fire, I quickly thanked her and left the room. I cried uncontrollably for around ten minutes. The emotions were totally overwhelming and directly parallel to the emotions of a young child. I sobbed for the loss of that spider eighteen years after the initial event. Afterwards I felt great relief, and now the fate of my spider does no more than spark the memory of this episode. Reliving the context of the situation had sparked off an unresolved emotion, which I had now, finally, resolved. As a child I hadn't accepted the fate of my spider and so it lay dormant within me.

Many psychologists believe that it is this type of 'repression' that leads to a great number of neuroses in the adult.

I think that it is helpful for actors to have

some basis on which to reference character traits, knowing the root of your character's traits, problems, barriers or neuroses, will aid you in your preparation.

## *Sub-Interactions*

Within interactions there can, and usually are, other interactions. It is easy to see this in the case of longer lasting interactions, but what about in one that takes a few seconds or a few minutes. Take for example Rhonda's dress buying. When Rhonda reaches the stage of Evaluation, many alternatives came to mind. Let's look at one of her thoughts.

**"I have a month to pay it off"**.

When the idea comes she has 'First Contact'. She soon realizes what exactly her idea is and has a resultant Need, which is to buy the garment. However, on entering the evaluation stage she reasons that;

**"I won't be able to get enough money in time"**.

Rhonda's 'commitment' is to think of something else, and so she goes on to postulate other alternatives and ways to raise the money. Rhonda has a chain of `sub-interactions' before resolving her main interaction with;

**"Damn, I'll buy it and work out how to pay for it later!"**

Note that Rhonda is having an interaction with herself, internal-interaction, paralleled somewhat in conventional acting theory as an 'internal conflict'.

The next Chapter deals with the theories tying together chains of interactions and the resultant manifestations.

## *Interaction Model Summary*

**_First Contact_** (Exert)
**Cue Focus** - (External/Internal)
**Emotional** - (Physiological Arousal)
**Intellectual** - (Stimulus)
**Body Weight** - (Up & Away/Forward)
**Voice Pitch** - (Higher)
**Breath Focus** - (In)
⇓

**_Realization & Acceptance_** (Recovery)
**Cue Focus** - (Internal)
**Emotional** - (Arousal Labeled - *Initial Emotion*)
**Intellectual** - (Perception)
**Body Weight** - (Down & Centered)
**Voice Pitch** - (Lower)
**Breath Focus** - (Out)
⇓

**_Need_** (Exert)
**Cue Focus** - (Internal)
**Emotional** - (Arousal/Emotion Reinforced)
**Intellectual** - (Primary Cognition)
**Body Weight** - (Up & Centered)
**Voice Pitch** - (Higher)
**Breath Focus** - (In)
⇓

**_Evaluation_** (Recovery)
**Cue Focus** - (Internal)
**Emotional** - (Arousal Label Questioned)
**Intellectual** - (Tertiary Cognition)
**Body Weight** - (Off-center/Shifting)
**Voice Pitch** - (Shifting)
**Breath Focus** - (In/Out Shifting)
⇓

**_Commitment_** (Exert)
**Cue Focus** - (External Response)
**Emotional** - (Arousal Decided – *Effective Emotion*)
**Intellectual** - (Decision made)
**Body Weight** - (Up & Forward)
**Voice Pitch** - (Higher)
**Breath Focus** - (In)

### Body Weight
Centered - Sure       Off-center - Unsure
Up - Outward Focus    Down - Inward Focus
Shifting - Unsure

### **Breath**
In - Outward Focus
Out - Inward Focus

## *Practical Exercises*

Firstly I want you to continue with the exercises from Chapter 1, these exercises are basic to your art so please keep them up!

Secondly I want you to go over the Interaction Summary. Make sure you understand the sequence of events and the properties therein.

Start to watch the interactions taking place in life; observe in life the stages of Interaction within yourself and others. Observe when people get 'stuck' in a stage. Try and see if you can tell when someone is re-labelling an emotion. Watch for signs of other peoples' 'Other', what are they reacting to? Notice if any of your friends or colleges' behaviour can be generally categorized as fitting predominantly into any one of the Interaction stages. If so, does this tell you anything about them? Be aware of body weight and how people move. Which part of their body do they lead with? Are they centred? How do they carry their weight? Become aware of your own physicality and how you carry yourself.
Observe how people stand. Are they leaning to the side, or standing straight up? Do they fidget? What does this tell you about their current state?

Well that's it for this Chapter, remember, keep working it's the consistency that will pay off!

**CHAPTER 3**

*Behaviourism, Trust & Sociological Spheres of Influence*

The Historical Environment

## Behaviorism

Behaviorism is the strand of psychology that adopts a straight cause and effect view on learning. There was an example of behaviorism in the first Chapter. Herman learnt that crying would bring mum, which would end in him getting attention. While the art/science of Psychology is a vast field of study with numerous valuable disciplines, I believe for the actor, Behaviouristic principals have the most to offer for character background and development.

First I need to give you a few basic definitions that we will work with. They will be simplistic because, as actors, we don't really need to delve too deeply in the psychological vernacular.

### Reinforcement

Reinforcement simply refers to a stimulus that makes a behavior **more** likely to occur in the future. For example if every time you performed on stage the audience cheered and applauded during the curtain call, then you are **more likely** to go onto stage in the future. The audiences' reaction *reinforced* the behavior of performing.

**Positive Reinforcement:** Positive Reinforcement refers to the onset of a reinforcing stimulus.

As in the Performing example previously, the audience, when cheering and clapping, gave you Positive Reinforcement. They gave you stimuli that made the likelihood of your behavior, performing, **more likely** to occur in the future.

**Negative Reinforcement:** Negative Reinforcement refers to the removal or termination of an aversive stimulus in order to make a behavior more likely to occur in the future.

For example, if every time your baby started crying you hugged and fed them, and consequently they stopped crying. The act of hugging and feeding your child was Negatively Reinforced by the termination of the crying, making it **more likely** that you will perform this behavior the next time your child cries.

*Punishment*

Punishment refers to a stimulus that makes a behavior **less likely** to occur in the future.

For example if every time you performed on stage the audience threw rocks at you, booed, hissed and then walked out, then you are **less likely** to go onto stage in the future. The audiences' reaction **punished** the Behaviour of performing.

**Positive Punishment:** Positive punishment refers to the onset of a punishing or aversive stimulus.

As in the Performing example previously, the audience, when booing and throwing rocks, gave you Positive Punishment. They gave you stimuli that made the likelihood of your behavior, performing, **less likely** to occur in the future.

**Negative Punishment:** Negative Punishment refers to the termination of rewarding stimuli, making the behavior **less likely** to occur in the future.

For example if you gain great satisfaction from watching your baby sleeping peacefully, and then you made a loud noise that woke them up in a fit of crying. The loud noise that terminated the rewarding stimulus, '*peacefully sleeping baby*', Negatively Punishes the Behaviour of making that noise. You would be **less** likely to make a loud noise in the same circumstances in the future.

Why do you need to know these terms and their meanings? These concepts and those discussed in this chapter are very helpful in understanding and helping to create the circumstances surrounding a characters background. It helps in the discovery of some of the driving forces behind the decisions that your character now makes.

Robert Carne
## Causal Chains

For Behaviorists there is a causal chain linking all actions. Here is an example of a possible causal chain ending in the destruction of the world. Frank, our resident megalomaniac, is our subject.

Baby Frank needs food → Frank's tummy hurts → Frank cries → Frank gets attention from parents → Frank is fed → Frank's crying is **reinforced** by the acquisition of food.

Three year old Frank gets into trouble and is sent to his room → Frank seeks attention from parents, Frank has learnt that crying brings about attention → Frank starts crying and screaming → Parents get frustrated at not being able to quieten Frank → Parents smack Frank giving him attention → Frank got the attention he was seeking and so crying/screaming is *reinforced* → Frank sensed his parents' frustration when hitting him and so associates hitting or smacking with frustration → hitting when frustrated is **reinforced** by his role models.

Franks brother, Tom, steals one of Frank's toys → Frank asks for his toy back → Tom refuses → Frank gets frustrated → Frank has learnt, from his parents, that hitting when frustrated produces positive results → Frank hits Tom → Tom starts crying → Parents arrive on the scene → Tom gets attention → Parents hit/smack Frank for hitting his brother → Toms crying is *reinforced* → Tom and Frank both learn that the biggest hitter wins → Parents have felt the need to have an effect on their child → Frank learns the need to effect people.

Frank is now an adult. Frank is in a pub → stranger abuses Frank → Frank gets frustrated and needs to effect the stranger → Frank has learnt to hit →

Stranger has also learnt to hit → Frank hits stranger first → Stranger falls to the ground → Frank relieves himself of the frustration and his need to effect → Winner is the stronger/bigger/more skilled or, first to strike is reinforced.

**Frank is now president of the U.S.A.**

An hostile country refuses to disarm and withdraw nuclear weapons from a border → Frank gets frustrated and needs to effect → Frank knows that the U.S.A. and the hostile country are more or less equal in arms → Frank thinks that if he hits first he could win the fight → Frank pushes a small red button and successfully destroys the world leaving 100% of actors out of work.

This example has been extreme to say the least. In between all the events that have been outlined are, for all intents and purposes, infinitely more events. To suggest that Frank's parents are to blame for Frank destroying the world would obviously be a bit unfair. However, the idea of cause and effect is a very useful one for the actor. If you are to play a character who decides to destroy the world you want to be familiar with their background and elements that could have had an influence on his/her decision – That which defines their character.

By stringing together chains of events throughout the characters life, the actor can get a feel for their motivations and how they re-label their emotions. This will also make it easier for the actor to re-label their emotions to be in line with that of the characters.

## *Operant Conditioning*

**Operant Conditioning** is the term used to describe a particular type of learning. The other main behaviouristic type is called **Classical Conditioning**, for our purposes however, we are going to concentrate on the former.

Operant Conditioning sees the consequences of a behavior reinforce or punish the preceding behavior.

For example, if you were to eat some form of exotic food that you had never tasted before and you were soon after violently sick, the preceding behavior - 'Eating the food' is **punished.** The consequences of your behavior, being violently sick, was **Positively Punishing** and so the behavior of eating that food becomes *less likely* to occur in the future.

Likewise if you had eaten that food and it tasted great and had no ill effects, the behavior - 'Eating the food' would have been **Positively Reinforced.** The consequences of your behavior, having a good, tasty meal, was **Positively Reinforced** and so the **preceding** behavior of eating that food becomes *more likely* to occur in the future.

There is one more aspect to the equation and that is;

The circumstances and 'Others' surrounding the behavior, 'sets the scene' for the possible expression of that behavior in future. So if you were to find yourself in a situation where that exotic food was in front of you again, it doesn't necessarily mean that what happened before will happen again, the scene is merely set for 'something' to happen. The potential is now there.

I'll put this theory into a practical context so that you can better understand the practicalities of these concepts.

You are playing the role of Katie, 21, in an upcoming film. In one particular scene you have to enter a bar that your ex-boyfriend frequents. Your ex-boyfriend was prone to violence and you did not part on good terms. He has hit you before; in fact he broke your nose in this very bar. You enter into the hotel ... and there he is staring at you. He is not smiling... Now, the scene is set for many potential outcomes.

As you approached the Hotel you need to be aware of the potential consequences of your characters' behavior – 'entering the hotel'. Your character may be apprehensive, skittish, downright scared, maybe she has the Initial Emotion of fear and the Effective Emotion' of fearless.

You enter the bar to see him. Now, your character doesn't know what is actually going to happen, however they are aware of the potential consequences of their being in this situation. This potential effects how they now deal with their 'Other', the ex-boyfriend.

So, the perceived possible consequences of a behavior, in a specific situation, will affect the way your character will interact within that environment.

We will look at this more towards the end of this Chapter in Sociological Spheres of Influence and also in the final Chapters where we bring everything together. Don't worry too much for now if your head is spinning a bit, give it time to sink in, live with it for a while, look at examples in life, there's no rush.

## *Trust*

Trust is a very important topic for the actor. You may have done acting or drama classes before where trust exercises were involved. Generally they involve activities like; Having some-one lead you around a room blindfolded. Falling backwards while some one catches you. Running blindfolded towards a wall where a few people will stop you.

These are some of the sorts of exercises that may be found in any given acting or drama class throughout the week. They are meant to teach you to trust the other actors by putting your full faith into them. Yes, they are valuable and they do help; however this is not the trust that I want to talk about.

I want to talk to you on a different level; maybe a philosophical level, maybe spiritual, maybe moral... Whatever your instinctive reactions to what is to follow are, I need you to keep an open mind, I need you to throw judgement out the window and cast a very objective eye into the light I'm about to shine. Try not to have any knee-jerk reactions, this is a hard topic to discuss and each person reading this will have a different view. After digesting it, try to find where it sits within your own moral framework. For now we are looking at it purely for acting purposes. I will be talking a bit around the topic to try and give you a flavour for what I'm attempting to convey.

I want you to think about what I call **Unconditional Trust**. Unconditional trust is when you trust the heart, the soul, the motivations, the very essence of humanity and its cultures. It is a trust that is *Unconditional*.

In our society we tend to have what I call **Behavioural Trust**. Behavioural trust is where you trust that someone's Behaviours are going to be 'true' to what you believe they should be, or what they've said they'll be.

Examples;

Most people trust that their partner will not sleep with other people. They trust that they will not engage in that Behaviour.

You may trust that in your 'trust' exercise in drama class the person behind you will catch you as you fall. Again, a trust in the other persons Behaviour.

You may trust that your partner will bring home milk that night; that your child will clean their room; that your daughter will be home by 10pm; that your staff won't steal pens from the office; that people won't drive over the speed limit or won't drink and drive; that your partner will remember your birthday; that your partner won't come home late drunk; that your wife will remember to put the garbage out... I dare say you get the picture!

All of these examples are illustrations of Behavioural Trust and as you all know, people fail in them all the time. We are, as they say, only human.

Our upbringings, our history, our own unique experiences of the world have played a huge role in shaping us as individuals. We talked in an earlier Chapter about the decisions we make defining the qualities of our character. What we now need to do is take our own personal history out of the equation and look objectively at a fictional character's personal history and **'Unconditionally Trust'** those decisions that come from their history.

I believe that most, if not all, of us are capable of killing given the right circumstances. Hopefully none of you will find yourselves in that situation. Perhaps you already have. We saw earlier in this Chapter how certain situations can set the scene for certain Behaviours given your historical experience in those environments. Now, given that we are all pretty much capable of killing, the only thing that separates you from some one who has killed (if you haven't already killed someone) is situational luck. They have found themselves in a situation where they would kill while you haven't.

Most of you reading this book will probably come from a background environment where love, education and a respect for life were nurtured. Maybe you don't fit into that category but let's, for the sake of argument, assume that you do. This being the case the number of situations where you'd actually take some ones life would be quite small and so the chance of you finding yourself in one of those situations is also slim. Let's look at a few possible situations where you **might** kill.

You come home one night to find your partner hanging from the ceiling, throat cut and a man raping your 6-year-old daughter on the floor nearby.

Walking home one night you are attacked by some one with a knife, it's you or them, one of you will die.

The world goes to war and you find yourself defending your hometown from a heavily armed opponent.

Note that these are all situations that will generally cut straight through your intellectual barriers and push straight into your physical/emotional self. (More on barriers in Chapter 4) If you are seeing your daughter being raped you are unlikely to stop and say;

"Excuse me, I think we should talk about this, I'm not happy about what you are doing."

You'll go straight to the physical and do something to stop them.

The chances are slim that you'll ever find yourself in one of those situations. But they do happen, and people do get killed and people just like you do the killing. So while the chances that you will one day actually kill someone may be small, for other people the circle of situations is wider because of their unique background.

Someone who comes from a violent family where a drunken mother or father would beat them may have a wider range of situations where they would kill. As they grow they are learning their behaviour from their *Others*, from the environment in which they live. It may be that they would kill if someone who was drunk picked them for a fight.

Maybe human life was treated as trivial in their historical environment, they may have grown up in a war torn country where killing and learning to kill was just a part of life. Do we blame them for that? Is it their fault where they were born?

So what does all this mean for the actor? It means that you need to approach each character you play from a position of 'Unconditional Trust', where you don't judge any of their behaviours but instead find that historical environment which made them that way and **LOVE THEM FOR IT.**

Let's say that in a script you play a character who beats their partner. You, as the actor, don't play an **'asshole'** that's how the audience may see them but that's not what you play. You play the character that watched a parent being beaten as a child, who learnt, through no fault of their own, that when you are frustrated with the opposite sex, that's what you do. That's what you know, that's how life goes, you don't know any different. So when you go onto stage and your character hits their partner, you are not playing an asshole, just someone who deals with life and situations in the manner in which they have learned and there is nothing '*wrong*' with that.

As a person you may find it inconceivable to rape someone, however in your acting career you might find yourself playing a rapist at some stage. Don't hate your character, love them, **trust** that what they are doing, the behaviour they are performing is for a real reason, it may not seem like a valid reason to you **but to them it is.** We are not to judge.

### *"There but for the grace of God go I"*

Find the Unconditional Trust within you. People will always fall short when judged against behavioural Trust. Trust that the motivations or needs behind the behaviours are valid and important to them. You may not like it, you may not agree with it, but then you have a choice of what you want to do about it.

Your partner may be unfaithful; Unconditional Trust would see you having faith in that persons 'soul', motivation, need; that they are on equal terms as a human with everyone else. They have found themselves in a situation where they would break a Behavioural Trust. They may have a small circle of circumstances where they would do that, or it may be large, depending on their background, but they have done this.

Trust that 'God' (or whatever you believe in) makes no 'bad' people, **we** only *choose* to define behaviours in terms of good and bad, right and wrong. So while you may not like what your partner has done, and in the end you may decide to leave them, that is your right and character choice, but do you need to judge them for it?

As I said before, you may look at this idea for yourself or not, up to you, however for the actor, Unconditional Trust is an important step for you to take. Each character should be viewed from a position of love and should not be judged for who they seem to be or what they have done. It is not your job as an actor to judge the characters that you play, that role belongs to the audience.

## *Transference of Effect*

Transference of Effect relates to the transference of an emotional response from one stimulus to another.

The most apparent and obvious use of this affect can be seen in advertising where it is used excessively. Sex sells!

> Gorgeous Woman ⇒ Emotional Response

Place gorgeous woman with a sleek sports car and theoretically there will be a Transference of Effect of the emotional response for the woman; onto the car. This is not to say that you now want to sleep with the car, but positive feelings translate across and so we enthusiastically run out and buy the car.

Beautiful Men, Women, sporting personalities etc, when associated with a product see a Transference of Effect from one to the other.

With this transference, in life, can often be an emotional re-labelling. We are generally in a constant state of trying to be comfortable; emotionally, physically, intellectually and spiritually. When we experience a 'negative' emotion we will often search the environment for a more positive emotional state, one that we are happier with.

It is often said that sometimes when hostages have finally been released from their captive, they have positive things to say about their captors. Even to the extent that they have gained a bond with them. The fear associated with this kind of event is not pleasant and so we search our environment for a cue onto which we can place a more 'positive' emotion.

Teachers, counsellors, doctors and psychologists, as well as many similar occupations, can be placed in very awkward situations when helping someone in trouble. When someone is in a situation where they need help or guidance, they are vulnerable emotionally. The strength of the unpleasant emotions, which are a result of their dilemma, can often be transferred and relabelled onto their helper. Thus many a student or client have found themselves sexually attracted to the person who has come to their aid. People in the aforementioned fields have a duty of care not to take advantage of this effect. Unfortunately, this is not always the case.

In film and television it also happens all the time; The hero and heroine are being pursued by the baddies, bullets raining around them, they come to a life or death situation with a decision to make. They stop look into each others eyes, kiss and then jump off the cliff into the river below...

The strength of the physiological state in a situation will be fairly well paralleled when transferred across and re-labelled. Bonds form between people who have been through strong ordeals. Generally speaking the more intense the ordeal the stronger the bond.

This transference and re-labelling is one of the most powerful weapons an actor can have, if they know how to wield it. In Chapter Seven I'm going to teach you a technique that, when learnt and perfected, will see a whole new world open before you. Don't read ahead now! Be patient. Complete this book in the order presented and all shall be revealed!

## *Sociological Spheres of Influence*

Sociological Spheres of Influence simply refers to those social circles, groups or clubs that we have and belong to. Our interests and those who inhabit our social lives affect the way we perceive things.

It is very likely that when we observe any given stimuli the people around us, apart from spatial observation differences, view, aesthetically, the same thing. However, even though the visual stimulation may be similar, the subjective perception can be vastly different, depending on the individual's historical sociological environment.

To illustrate this point let's observe a beach scene through the eyes of a number of different people. Firstly let me point out that visually the scene is more or less identical. Each person views waves curling and breaking near the shore, people sunbaking, birds out to sea, etc.

The first person to view this theoretical beach belongs to the local fishing club and is a very enthusiastic angler. Most of their friends enjoy fishing and they all compete regularly in tournaments. So, what does this person view?

As they look out, certain elements within the environment will be more salient to them than others. This selectivity is due to one of their Sociological Spheres of Influence. Being an angler influences their 'Perception' and 'Evaluation' of the scene. This person notices that there is a deep hole not far off shore. There is a channel that runs from this hole out to sea.

Our angler sees a possible good fishing spot for the coming weekend competition. Looking out they also notice that there are a number of birds diving at the surface of the water and conclude that they are most likely feeding on the remnants of fish being eaten by larger pelagic species, another good sign. Observing that the tide is almost low and given the present time and day, the weekend's tides should be favourable for fish. A strong current is viewed and so a heavy sinker will be needed.

We can see that what seemed to be a relatively simple scene has held a lot of significance for our angler.

The second person to view our beach scene is a surfer. They too notice the hole and the channel but for a different reason. This channel may mark an easy path for them to paddle out. They notice that the waves are breaking from left to right, the type of waves and the probable ride length. They also see the strong current but again have a different motive. The strong current may make paddling difficult and if they are caught in a strong rip, they may be taken out to sea. Again this is a reflection of one of their sociological spheres of influence.

A marine biologist, a sunbaker, a body-surfer, a person whose father is presently lost out at sea, an ice-cream seller, a life guard, a swimmer, a 'Greeny', a rapist, a young child, a person brought up in the country, or even an actor studying Sociological Spheres of Influence will all bring their own sociological background to their perception of the scene.

In any given situation, individuals bring their own experiences and past sociological environments to their present perception. When creating a character, the characters previous environments and sociological influences, will greatly effect how they react in any given circumstance.

Sociological Spheres of Influence are important because people will exist in different realities in the same place. If two characters within a play are looking at a bunch of flowers, the emotion of the two could be vastly different if one person has just been to a funeral and the other a wedding. The social content of their recent past will effect how they react in the present, as will distant experiences. Because you have your own Sociological Spheres of Influence, you need to be aware of them so that they don't influence your enacted roles.

Items or props can also hold spheres of sociological influence. For example;

I will have a different reaction to someone breaking a pen that I found last week, than if they were to break a pen given to me by my mother who just passed away. The pen has been encoded into memory sociologically with my mother and will bring up emotions encoded with her. The specific emotion will be dependant on the current environment and the environment of encoding. Also, any other encoding relevant to the pen may also effect the emotion. For example;

I may have been given the pen as a gift for my Final Year Exams. I may have completed all of my School and University exams using that pen. This encoding, coupled with it being broken, will have an effect on my current emotional state. While considering what has happened, I may remember that my mother borrowed this pen when she signed her last will and testament. All of these memories may come flooding back and will have an effect on my current emotional state. The other person's reaction to breaking the pen will, in turn, also effect my emotions. If they are extremely sorry for what has happened my emotion will be different than if they break down laughing.

## Emotionally Charged Props

'Emotionally charging' a prop can be a very useful tool for the actor. By giving the current environment a past, scenes acted within can be infinitely enhanced. For example;

If you are enacting a scene in a play and the setting is your bedroom. If all the sets and props are merely sets and props to you, how are you going to truthfully 'live' in the scene? By knowing that the chair in the corner was a wedding present from your mother-in-law, and the painting on the wall was done by your four year old daughter, Samantha, and knowing that you bought the mantle clock from a little antique shop in the south of France will enhance the 'life' in the situation for the actor. If during one performance the clock is accidentally smashed, your reaction to it must be 'truthful' within the environment of the play. The audience will know immediately it was a mistake if you don't react consistently in character.

We will look at the process of emotionally charging props in Chapter 7.

### Objects and Items

These are the two terms we will be using to define whether we have a history with a prop or not.

**Objects**, for our purposes, are props with which our character **has no** personal history.

**Items**, for our purposes, are props with which our character **has** a personal history.

Our characters will react to objects in no personal terms, unless; It reminds us of an item or the type of object holds a specific reference within our character's Sociological Spheres of Influence.

For example; Sam, our surfing character, sees a surfboard atop a station wagon while on holidays in the middle of Australia. This surfboard may not look at all like her own board, or any that she has come across.

But because of her Sociological Spheres of Influence she has a personal reaction to it.

**"I can't wait to get home and back on my board!"**

Items, however, have all been emotionally charged to a greater or lesser degree, within the context of our historical environment.

Items can greatly assist in your performance in a couple of ways.

> 1) They give you, **the actor**, strong material ties into a characters own unique history. They are the 'Others' that can help you bring meaning, substance and weight to a scene. I know you have probably heard the cliché;

"All an actor needs is a bare room and an audience".

Romantically that sounds nice, but in training give yourself as many physical 'items' as you need to help your performance, to help bring your character to life. After all, the busy café scene is not going to be shot in an empty room, why rehearse in one?

> 2) They give the **audience** strong material ties into a characters history. You may, in a movie, see a child with a Teddy Bear throughout much of the film. The child loves that Bear and so the audience grows to love it.

If during the final scenes there is an earthquake and we see that the Bear is lying next to a pile of rubble, it affects us because of its sociological and emotional tie with the child. Then, in the final scene, after the quake is finally over and the cleanup has started, we see a fireman pickup the Bear, look off screen and say;

"Is this yours?"

Then cut to a wide shot revealing the child and her mother as the child takes the Bear into her arms – We have hope for the future. We feel for the child, and the bond that exists between her and her Teddy Bear, strengthens our emotion.

So Items help the actor bring the character to life and they help the audience find the life in the character.

## *Practical Exercises*

1) Start looking at cause and effect in your life. See the causal chains and watch for Operant Conditioning being played out.

2) Talk with friends and associates and get their views on trust. How do they use, abuse and define trust?

3) Start to identify in life stimuli that you find, Punishing or Reinforcing. See how they differ, or are similar, to other people's perceptions.

4) Look for examples in advertising, and in life in general, of Transference of Effect.

5) Identify your own Sociological Spheres of Influence, past and present.

6) When out and about look at scenes, like the beach, be aware of your own perceptions and what is salient for you and then put yourself into another characters' shoes. How may they view the scene? What is salient for them? What were their spheres of influence that led them to this perception?

7) Look at things in your house and think about the emotional attachment that you have with them. How would you feel if you lost something? What if your house was burnt to the ground, what are the two items you'd most like to survive?

# CHAPTER 4

# *Vulnerability and Status*

### The Powers we Wield

## Vulnerability

Vulnerability is a very powerful aspect of any character. It is through vulnerability that a character can reveal very basic human emotions, emotions that can tear at the hearts of an audience. Vulnerability is defined, for our purposes as;

### 'Open to Attack'

If we are 'open to attack' then we are 'vulnerable'. Something to keep in mind, which is very important, is, 'open to attack' is **by choice**. Conscious or otherwise, there is a choice. The reason this is so important will become apparent later in this Chapter when we look at Status. As a general rule we choose to protect those areas that we feel open to attack on, so for the most part in our daily lives we choose not to be vulnerable.

People are vulnerable in different areas to varying degrees. When some-one attacks your vulnerabilities you can either open yourself up to them (become vulnerable to) or put up defensive barriers to protect yourself.

If a character *doesn't* put up any emotional defenses, (done by changing the initial emotion), to an attack on their vulnerabilities, then what the character is left with is a 'truthful' primary emotion being expressed. This 'truthful' emotion, or the protection of, will move an audience to tears, or rage, or to any other emotion the actor/director focuses on.

## Vulnerability Traits

We will look at four types of vulnerabilities that have an effect on our behavior. These vulnerabilities will be expressed for the moment at the extremes, no-one is totally one or another, but lie somewhere on a continuum. The four vulnerabilities are made up of two continuums; The Self and The Social.

## *The Self Continuum*

The first two vulnerabilities, which lie on 'The Self' continuum, are called;

**Intellectual Vulnerability**
And
**Emotional Vulnerability**

## *Intellectual Vulnerability*

An Intellectually Vulnerable person is someone who feels a need to protect his or her intellect, someone who doesn't have strong cognitive capabilities for defense in a certain situation and so protects in a physical/emotional way.

The historical environment of an Intellectually Vulnerable person would, as a general rule, see a modest to low level of education, possibly from a lower socioeconomic background and maybe with a family history of strong physical or emotional confrontation.

An Intellectually Vulnerable person would seek to construct a protective barrier formed from their Emotional or Physical self.

Children, for the most part, start out as Intellectually Vulnerable. The child cries, stamps their feet, hits and generally deals with confrontation in an emotional and physical way. As they grow up they learn and develop their intellectual barriers and so become more adept at intellectually confrontation, a state more widely accepted in our culture.

As mentioned, a poorly educated person brought up in a lower socio-economic area would possibly be Intellectually Vulnerable. If a college student were to start insulting them with words outside of their experience then our Intellectually Vulnerable person would be more likely to defend with what they feel more comfortable with, their strength, their emotional or physical barrier. They may go from an 'Initial' emotion of hurt, to an 'effective' emotion of anger and so punch the student to defend their vulnerable side.

**Intellectually Vulnerable**
⇓
**Emotional or Physical Barrier**

*Emotional Vulnerability*

An Emotionally Vulnerable person is one who needs to protect their emotions or physical and so seeks to construct a protective barrier within their intellect.

In our current culture, Emotional Vulnerability is generally more accepted than Intellectual Vulnerability. From our early years we are trained to:

"**Think before you act**"
"**Don't be a sook**"
"**Take three deep breaths**"
"**Count to ten**"
"**Use your head and think next time**"
"**Relax and calm down**"

Sound familiar? It's very rare that you would be told;

"**Cry more**"
"**Just punch him out and think about it later**"
"**Don't relax, you don't have to take that from her!**"

So, as a general rule we preliminarily put up an Intellectual barrier, or screen, to protect our vulnerable emotions rather than allowing emotions to rule our behaviors.

A person with a good education, brought up in a very loving and caring environment, would most likely be emotionally sensitive; given the trust and care that has surrounded them. This being the case then the capacity for them to be hurt emotionally is increased.

In order to protect their emotions in the world they look to their intellect for the protection of their emotionally vulnerable side.

For example, take two hypothetical Hotels. The first is set in an environment or area that sees much of its demographic being Intellectually Vulnerable. Since this demographical group protects more with a physical/emotional barrier, there is a good chance that a confrontation will be negotiated in a physical altercation.

However the second hotel, which is set in an affluent area where the patrons are more likely to be Emotionally Vulnerable, would see any confrontation more likely to be settled in a diplomatic way.

We don't need to look far to see this sort of thing happening on a global scale. There are other cultures throughout the world that tend to be more Intellectually Vulnerable. These countries are much more ready to resort to violence and warfare to resolve differences than countries who are more Emotionally Vulnerable, who would rather settle differences diplomatically.

There are of course numerous cases when a country, has resorted to retaliatory violence against another country even though they are generally of the Emotionally Vulnerable inclination. In many of these cases the aggressive attacking group have got through the intellectual barriers of the other group, or country, and have forced them to act on their vulnerable side, their physical and emotional.

The September 11 attack on the twin towers in New York 2001 is one very salient example. The attackers on America cut through the Intellectual Barriers of the country, America wasn't inclined to use diplomacy or any other form of Intellectual response, instead they struck back.

## Emotionally Vulnerable
⇓
## Intellectual Barrier

### *'Self' Vulnerabilities Interacting*

If, for example our Intellectually Vulnerable person and our Emotionally Vulnerable person were in conflict;

The **Emotionally Vulnerable Person** would most likely try and talk their way out of it, rather than go with their vulnerable emotions/physical.

The **Intellectually Vulnerable Person** would most likely try to keep it on an emotional or physical level, protecting their vulnerable intellect.

If two Emotionally Vulnerable people were arguing then the conflict would most likely stay on an intellectual level, unless one party managed to break through the others Intellectual Barrier and thus force them to protect on an emotional/physical level.

The way in which to breach a barrier is to confront it with a stimulus that the barrier cannot withstand. Maybe one particular Emotionally Vulnerable person can deal intellectually with personal insults, but when someone insults their partner they are no longer prepared or able to protect at that level, the barrier is breached and so they resort to the emotional or physical.

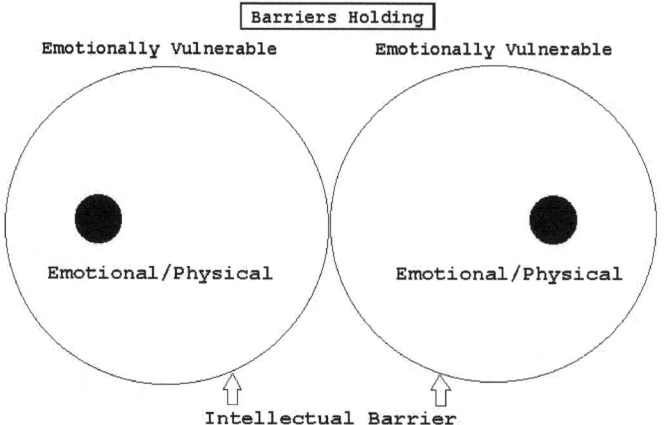

**Barriers Holding**

Emotionally Vulnerable     Emotionally Vulnerable

Emotional/Physical     Emotional/Physical

⇧ ⇧
Intellectual Barrier

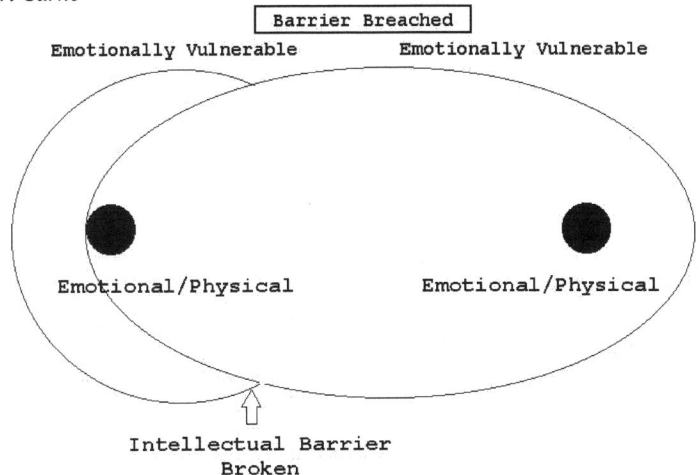

```
         ┌─────────────────┐
         │ Barrier Breached│
Emotionally Vulnerable    Emotionally Vulnerable
```

[Diagram: Two overlapping ellipses, each containing a black dot labeled "Emotional/Physical", with an arrow pointing up to the intersection labeled "Intellectual Barrier Broken"]

Intellectual Barrier
Broken

Likewise if two Intellectually Vulnerable people were to argue it would be more likely to lead to a physical fight or an excessively emotional scene. And if, in the end, that doesn't resolve their differences they may just be forced to talk about it.

## Characters & 'Self' Vulnerabilities

Characters' vulnerabilities can be very important to the actor for they will help determine the re-labeling of the emotion and what effect it will have on the Evaluation Stage of Interaction.

For example; An Emotionally Vulnerable person with a Primary Emotion of fear would most likely try to re-label their fear as 'cautious', or some other 'intellectually' driven state.

Herman, our hero, sees Tony, legendary Martial artist and brother of Rhonda, in a Hotel. History tells us that Tony doesn't approve of Herman seeing his little sister. Tony sees Herman. Herman feels fear. But hey, this is a public place, he's allowed to be here and what is Tony going to do with all these people around anyway?!

Herman has intellectually made himself more 'comfortable', he has justified his fear away. His intellectual barriers are holding.

As Herman watches, Tony pulls out a knife and starts running towards him. Herman's Intellectual barriers are breached, fear sets in as he runs for his life!!

An Intellectually Vulnerable person in the same situation would be more likely to re-label their fear as rage, or some other 'effectual' emotion. When they first saw Tony they may have attacked him, or immediately ran away.

Protecting your vulnerable areas is merely one way that allows us to cope in the world. Tertiary Cognition is where the decision, conscious or unconscious, is made to protect your vulnerable traits with an effective barrier.

### *In the Interaction Model*

Within the Interaction Model we can see, as a general guide, where the focus lies for an Intellectually or Emotionally Vulnerable person.

An **Intellectually Vulnerable** person protects themselves with their Emotions/Physical, and so their main focus in the interaction would most likely lie within the Need Stage (The highest area of active initial emotion).

An **Emotionally Vulnerable** person protects themselves with their Intellect, and so their main area of focus would most likely lie in the Evaluation stage of Interaction (The highest area of Cognitive functioning)

For example; Joan, after being discovered kissing Herman passionately in a corner, finds herself under a barrage of insults from Rhonda. In the Need stage Joan finds she has a **need** to hurt Rhonda;

If Joan were an **Intellectually Vulnerable** person she would most likely focus on the 'Need' stage of the interaction and try to attack Rhonda emotionally or physically. Since Joan's physical/emotional barriers are her strongest defense, this would be her first port of call for the protection of her vulnerable intellect. She would probably physically attack Rhonda or start screaming at her.

If Joan were an **Emotionally Vulnerable** person she would most likely find her focus lying in the 'Evaluation Stage' of the interaction and so she would focus on defending or attacking on an intellectual level. Since Joan's Intellectual barriers are her strongest defense, in this case, this would be her first port of call for protection of her vulnerable emotions. She would probably talk to Rhonda, trying to calm her down, pointing out that Herman has not made a commitment to any one person. Generally reasoning with Rhonda to avoid any emotional or physical confrontation.

Note that Joan as an Intellectually Vulnerable person would be more likely to continue with the Initial Emotion than would Joan as an Emotionally Vulnerable person.

Also, an Intellectually Vulnerable person would be more likely to re-label a strong emotion with another strong emotion, whereas the Emotionally Vulnerable person would try to Intellectually pacify the intensity of the salient emotion.

## *The Social Continuum*

The second two areas, which lie on The 'Social' continuum, are called;

**Social Vulnerability**
And
**Personal Vulnerability**

## Social Vulnerability

A Socially Vulnerable person is someone who feels open to attack, or is uncomfortable, in a **social context**. The Socially Vulnerable are more secure, or comfortable, dealing in a personal context.

A Socially Vulnerable person would seek refuge, or safety, within themselves, or by themselves when faced with a confronting or troubling situation.

For example if a Socially Vulnerable person had just split up with their partner, then they would be more likely to go off on their own, into a personal context, to recover, than to go to others for help.

A person who is a 'loner', or a Hermit, would be considered towards the Socially Vulnerable end of the continuum. At a party the Socially Vulnerable person would steer clear of the crowds, preferring to be with only a couple of friends or by themselves.

**Socially Vulnerable**
⇓
**Seeks Personal Environment for comfort and recovery**

## Personal Vulnerability

At the other end of this continuum we have the Personally Vulnerable people.

A Personally Vulnerable person is someone who feels open to attack, or is uncomfortable, in a **personal context**. The Personally Vulnerable are more secure, or comfortable, dealing in a social context, around other people.

A Personally Vulnerable person would seek refuge, or safety, within a social environment, preferring to be with friends or around other people.

For example if a Personally Vulnerable person had just split up with their partner, then they would be more likely to go over to their friends place, or have people come to them. They feel better able to cope and recover with other people around, rather than being by themselves.

At a party the Personally Vulnerable person is very social and out-going. The Personally Vulnerable person feels safer and more comfortable when interacting with other people.

### *Personally Vulnerable*
⇓
### Seeks Social Environment for recovery and comfort

**Note:** No-one is really at either extreme of the continuum, but rather they generally lean towards one end or the other. Individuals in different situations also see differing vulnerabilities. You may be very Socially Vulnerable around strangers but Personally Vulnerable when with friends. Or Socially Vulnerable when your cat dies but Personally Vulnerable when a close relative passes away.

The time and place of an event can also have a big influence on your current vulnerabilities. You may be generally Personally Vulnerable but when menstruating become Socially Vulnerable at that time. The specifics of any situation, coupled with what you bring to it, ie, tired, menstruating, broken arm, 'recent events', etc..., will all greatly effect the vulnerabilities you display in any given environment.

## *In the Interaction Model*

A Socially Vulnerable person, when looking for 'cues', (see Interaction model) searches for them 'internally'. This inward focus is, again, their source of refuge.

When looking at the Interaction Model we can also generalize and hypothesize about the likely physical aspects of a Socially Vulnerable person. Have a look at the Interaction model and see what generalizations you can make.

A Personally Vulnerable person, when looking for 'cues', (again see Interaction model) search for them externally. This external focus is their source of refuge. Again, with a Personally Vulnerable person, we can draw out some generalizations about their physical aspects by referring to the Interaction model. See what generalizations you can make.

## *When Two Continuums Collide*

The four vulnerabilities we have looked at are;

**Intellectual**
**Emotional**
**Social**
**Personal**

The two Continuums we looked at were;

**Intellectual** ⇐--------------⇒ **Emotional**
**Social**  ⇐------------⇒ **Personal**

These two continuums cross at some point to give the following four combinations which help enhance our understanding of the vulnerabilities. The four variations give us likely actions on 'Self', (**Emotional ⇔ Intellectual**) and on a 'Social', (**Social ⇔ Personal**) level.

Continuum 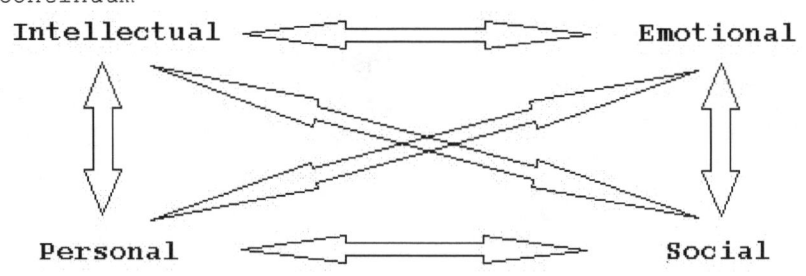
**Intellectual** ⇐=========⇒ Emotional

⇕                                    ⇕

**Personal** ⇐=========⇒ Social
Continuum

The first combination of the two continuums is;

*Intellectual/Social Vulnerability.*

A person leaning towards the intellectual and social ends of the continuums would seek refuge within their emotions and in a **personal** context.

For example, if an Intellectually/Socially Vulnerable person had split up with their partner then they would probably go off by themselves and cry.

**They are seeking recovery in an Emotional/Personal way.** The second variation is:

*Intellectual/Personal Vulnerability*

A person at these ends of the continuums would seek their refuge within their **emotions** and in a **social** context.

For example, if an Intellectually/Personally Vulnerable person had just split up with their partner they would probably seek out a friend and cry on their shoulder.

**They are seeking recovery in an Emotional/Social way.** The third variation is;

*Emotional/Social Vulnerability*

A character who is inclined towards these ends would seek comfort and within their **intellect** and in a **personal** context.

Again utilizing the previous example of splitting up with a partner, the Emotionally/Socially Vulnerable person would probably go off on their own and try to puzzle out what went wrong.

**They are seeking recovery in an Intellectual/Personal way.** The Final Variation is:

### Emotional/Personal Vulnerability

A person who tends towards these ends would seek refuge within their **intellect** and in a **social** context.

If the Emotional/Personally Vulnerable person breaks up with their partner then they would probably seek out a friend and try and rationalize with them what went wrong.

**They are seeking their recovery in an intellectual/social way.**

## Vulnerability History

What is the causal chain that precedes vulnerability traits? If a character is Emotionally/Socially Vulnerable, you need to know how your character came to be that way to provide a better background preparation to work from.

The script is the first place to look when searching for clues as to the characters vulnerabilities. The actual script analysis and character development will be looked at in more depth in a later Chapter. For now let's have a look at a couple of examples of possible causal chains linking specific vulnerability types.

**Example 1:**

**Scott is a Personally/Intellectually Vulnerable person.**

When Scott was a child he was never very good at school, he genetically lacked a high intelligence and his young childhood environment was not very stimulating. Throughout his life Scott was told that he was below average. The education system, in all its wisdom, decided to label children from a young age in terms of IQ. Since people look to their environment for answers, Scott's answer was that he would never amount to much. (In Psychological terms this is known as the 'self fulfilling prophesy', when a person adopts the label put on by society) Scott now thought of himself as 'not much of a person' and so sought his safety or refuge within a social context. Going to the social scene helped protect his Personal Vulnerability.

And so Scott grew up being loud, extroverted, rebellious and affectacious. He had a gang of like-minded friends at school who would all support each other.

Scott and his 'gang' put all their problems into the environment. If they weren't going well at school, to make themselves feel better, they would tease children that were going well to keep their own vulnerability safe.

If a child started to tease Scott about his school marks, Scott would resort to either emotional insults or force as a means of protecting his vulnerable intellect. Often his social gang would back him up. In short, Scott sought refuge from his lack of personal confidence within the social environment and utilized his aggression and physicality to protect himself from an intellectual attack. His gang gave him safety from his Personal Vulnerability.

**Example 2:**

**Jennifer is a Socially/Emotionally Vulnerable person.**

Jennifer was always a shy child, her parents, while very loving, did not give her too many opportunities to play with other children. As an only child, Jennifer would spend many hours at home by herself playing with dolls, her train set and coloring pictures. From an early age Jennifer never really had much social practice, and when the family did go to a social event, Jennifer would prefer to stay close to mum, or go and sit by the water alone.

Jennifer's parents, Brad and Janet, are a very loving couple, Jennifer is never short of a hug and the family unit is very strong.

As a teenager Jennifer, while having friends, likes her own time that she usually spends studying or playing the piano.

In her past Jennifer has not had the opportunity to forge strong social skills, her strengths lie in her ability to deal and cope on her own. As such in times of trouble Jennifer prefers to be alone.

Jennifer's loving background has seen her become an emotionally sensitive woman, and with her excellent education, she successfully manages to protect her vulnerable emotions with steady intellectual barriers.

**Quick Re-Cap**

In the previous Chapter we looked at Behaviorism, the causal chains linking events or traits, and Sociological Spheres of Influence, those social groups who have influence our lives and our current perceptions.

In this Chapter we have looked at 'Vulnerabilities', we have also looked at causal chains linking vulnerabilities to their past. We now turn our attention to one major way these vulnerabilities influence the interaction of every day life. This raising, lowering, extending and shrinking of vulnerability barriers is known as Status.

## *Status*

### *Interactional Status*

Status does not exist in a vacuum and therefore exists purely within the interaction. Now read this very closely, it may sound weird but stay with me.

The **more vulnerable** the person, **the *higher* the status**.

### The *less* vulnerable, the *lower* the status.

If a character is totally barrier free, ie, allowing themselves to be effected fully, intellectually, emotionally, personally, socially and spiritually, then they are making an interactional bid for high status. Because they are giving themselves to their environment, they are totally open to any sort of attack.

The area, which houses barriers for vulnerability protection, is called, 'Personal Space'. Personal Space, as an identity of its own, will be discussed in detail in the next Chapter.

To illustrate the idea of, the more vulnerable, the higher the status, I shall draw a parallel using two material subjects - military fortifications.

In this example both forts are about to be attacked by an enemy. The first fort, 'Fort Barricade', decides to fight to the death and so puts up as many barriers as it can. The second fort, 'Fort Open', decides to allow the enemy to do whatever they want with the fort and its people.

'Fort Open' puts up no defenses and invites the enemy to invade. Who has the higher status? Who is the more vulnerable? Obviously 'Fort Open' with no barriers is the more vulnerable and therefore of higher status. At this point most readers will probably be shifting in their seat. (yes that is a sign of Evaluation) The usual question put to me by students is;

"But if 'Fort Open' is going to be destroyed, how can they be the higher status?".

Fair question. To start in answering that question, the enemy feels a need to effect the fort, ie, they want to destroy it. Now by putting up defenses 'Fort Barricade' is in effect saying;

"I *can* be hurt, I don't want to be hurt".

Because 'Fort Barricade' has told the enemy that they don't want to be hurt, in being hurt they have not only lost the physical battle but also the Interactional status battle.

However, 'Fort Open' by offering no resistance is freely giving the area away. There is no Physical Battle to lose. If the enemy destroys it, it is their own loss because it was given to them in the first place. They have destroyed their own Fort; anything the enemy does is done with the permission of 'Fort Open'. The enemy cannot win an Interactional Status conflict if 'Fort Open' does not give them that conflict. The enemy, however, who has expressed a **Need** to affect, has lowered themselves by this need. As 'Fort Open' cannot be affected, ie, they ***allow*** all that happens, the enemy is destined to lose the Interactional Status even though they now have the Fort.

At this point I must add that this is a concept that generally takes a while to fully grasp and be able to distinguish and generalize in other situations. We'll now look at how this concept works in a personal interaction.

Take a bar room fight. Tony, our legend martial artist, picks a fight with Herman. Herman does not want to fight and so offers no resistance. Tony proceeds to beat Herman to a pulp. Despite what you may feel is logically right, it is Herman who has the higher status. By putting up no resistance Herman is giving himself totally to Tony, and so when Tony beats him up, Tony is abusing what has been given to him. Herman gave himself to Tony and Tony destroyed what was his.

In the film **'Crimson Tide'** there is a scene when Gene Hackman's character punches Denzel Washington's character a couple of times. When you watch the scene you will see what I mean. Even though Denzel Washington ends up bleeding, he maintains the higher status throughout the scene. His character has not found the **'Need'** to affect Gene Hackman, while Hackman's character has developed a great need to affect Denzel Washington.

## *Control*

Control is a major part of status. Controlling a situation is seen as high status. Along with situational control, the lack of 'needing to effect', is also high status.

A person who 'needs' to control a given situation is of a lower status than someone who doesn't 'need' to control the situation.

For example, let's say that your best friend has rung you up and asked you to go to a movie. To start, your friend is giving you a higher status because they 'need' something from you and they are trying to control the situation. (Control being that they are attempting to control your behavior). You, on the other hand, are in control of the situation because you can say - **"Yes" or "No"**

Or you could even just hang up on them. Also, you don't 'need' to try to control the situation because you already do. Anytime someone asks something of you, they are giving you the higher status because they need or want something from you. You now have the power to even out the status, fall lower in status or raise yourself in status.

Lowering your status could be achieved by giving the control back to them;

**YOU**
"I'll go if you want to go"

Accepting the offer and giving something in return may achieve an even status.

**YOU**
"Yes, I'd love to go."

Raising yourself in status may be achieved by taking full control of the situation.

**YOU**
"No we'll go bowling tonight instead"

While all three responses have seen you make a bid for status, the third situation has seen you make a bid for higher status. It may or may not be successful. Your best friends response will decide whether or not you are successful;

**Successful**

**Best Friend**
"Oh, okay"

**Not Successful**

**Best Friend**
"No thanks."
(Hangs up)

Note: Inflections and physicalities in both examples may change the status.

## *Manipulating Status*

Using a person's name is a good example of one way to manipulate status.

Whenever you use someone else's name you are putting them into a higher position of status because you want something from them. They then have the power and the control over whether you get it or not. This idea goes as basic as simple acknowledgment.

For example if your name is 'Tanya' and someone says, **"Tanya"**... to you, then they want to ask you something, or at least want you to acknowledge their existence. You have control over the situation. You can ignore them, answer yes, no or do anything you'd like because they have given you control. If you turn around and say, **"Yes"**... then you have raised them in status because you are acknowledging them and want to know what they want to say.

One way to find out who thinks *highly* of you is to notice who of your friends use your name often.

**Note:**

Note the use of **highly** in the previous paragraph. Status is built into the language, to think highly of someone is to raise them in status. The physicality of height supports high status. Some other examples in our language, which allude to status with a focus on the proximetrics are;

'Her Royal *Highness*'
'The *Lowly* Peasant'
"That was a *low* act"
'The *High* Court'
'The *High* Priest'
"You *low* down ..."
'*High* Society'
'A *high* point in life'
'A *low* point in life'

Status in Proximetrics can also be seen in the physical relationships, ie, higher, lower, off-center or centered. For example, if we look at two people facing towards each other, eyes closed, with one being notably taller than the other. Within the relationship one seems to be higher status than the other.

We will look further into the Status within proximetrics in another Chapter.

Getting back to what I was saying, one way to find out who thinks highly of you is to notice how often your friends use your name.

If you can remember your school days, or are still in them, you would have had a group that you 'hung' around with. In this group there usually would have been a hierarchy of some sort, ie, a charismatic type who everybody wanted to talk to, or be acknowledged by (High Status), some who were only slightly lower in status, and others who just sort of 'hung around' (Low Status).

If you are lucky enough to still be in school, or care to try and remember your school social environment, then you may notice that the less 'charismatic', or lower status types would use the 'charismatic', or higher status types names in conversation a lot more than the other way around.

If for example the leader of the group was Tom Jones, the lower status people in the group would say things like;

"Tom what do you want to play?"<br>
or<br>
"Tom are you coming to maths?"<br>
or<br>
"Tom what do you think of Tanya?"

While on the other hand Tom would most likely have answered not using their name, and even if he wanted to ask someone something he would be more likely to say;

"Are you guys playing?"<br>
or<br>
"Hey, are you coming to maths?"<br>
or<br>
"What do you think of Tanya?"

Name manipulation for status can do a couple of things. You can either raise their status or you can lower it.

For example if a friend of yours has a low self esteem and you want to try to raise it, then, by raising their status you will make them feel better about themselves, make them feel more important, more 'in control'. And so by using their name when talking to them you can help them.

On the other hand, if you are a teacher who gets your kicks out of power tripping over your students, then you can further isolate yourself and make them feel low by not using their name at all. This is one way to guarantee that the student is on their way to feeling worthless. (No, I do not recommend this.)

Cast your mind back to your school days and think of two teachers, one being a teacher that the class respected and the other one that held no respect from the class at all. What did the two teachers do that was different? Well I'll give you a clue, as a general rule one would have been a master of status. Yes, you guessed it, the teacher you most likely had the most respect for, and thus usually made the best teacher, was in fact a master of status.

This teacher could make their status lower than yours; Have a joke on them-selves, admit their own mistakes, accept that they are not perfect, or; Make their status equal to yours; Talk to you as an equal, have a laugh with you. And they could raise their status above yours; In controlling the class, quieting the class when too noisy or reprimanding when someone went too far. Sound familiar?

Then there were three other types of teacher.

The teachers who kept higher status at all times; Never admitting a mistake, looking down on everyone, treating the class as 'lesser' people and generally not 'caring' for the student's needs or emotions. Always going for high status. Often using the 'fear factor'.

Then there were those teachers who were low status; They were teachers who showed lots of need. Need to control the class, need to do well, need to affect the class. These teachers often, while trying to gain a higher status, would physically and vocally portray low status. High voices, shifting of weight, generally uncertain and with a great need.

And there were those teachers who just wanted to be one of the gang and be of equal status; Didn't control the class, just let them do what they wanted, made a few jokes. Maybe even had a few jokes on some of the students. In general they never really asserted any authority, but never really gave any either.

Focus and the enlarging and shrinking of Personal Space has a great deal to do with status. A person, who is totally vulnerable to another person, and thus high status, has let this other person within the walls of their Personal Space. This is just like the fort example where one fort offered no resistance and so allowed the enemy within their 'space'.

Outward focus, as shall be discussed further in the next Chapter, expands the Personal Space, while the inward focus shrinks the Personal Space. As a general rule the person who has the larger personal space, thus encompassing the other person, is the more vulnerable and so of a higher status. Likewise the person, whose focus is inward with a shallow Personal Space, is less vulnerable and so lower status.

Similar observations can be made when viewing the physical as either centered or off-center. The off-centered position is characterized within the interaction model in Evaluation and so is an unsure stage and has an inward focus. If you are unsure or are evaluating then you need something, ie, the answer, otherwise you wouldn't be evaluating. Since you feel the need to find an answer, and your focus is inward, this illustration of low vulnerability puts this physical position in the lower status bracket. The centered position, most prominent in Realization/Acceptance, is seen in the interaction model as a 'knowing' position and so lacks the 'need' of the off-centered position. This 'knowing' gives the centered position a high status.

Other physical traits pertaining to status are in the formation of barriers and the direct manifestations of `re-labeled' weight distribution.

For example, hands by the sides would be classified as high status because this leaves the body open and vulnerable.

Hands folded across the chest would be seen as low status because the person in question is protecting themselves, putting up a barrier, and thus possible to hurt.

Hands placed behind the head are an open and vulnerable position and so high status. However, quite often legs crossed and a leaning back in the chair accompanies this position of hands behind the head. In this example we see a contradiction in vulnerabilities between the hands and the legs. To evaluate fully we need to look not only at the physical but also at the total picture.

Let's first look at the upper part of the body. Firstly the body weight is away from the center giving an evaluation or unsure 'feel' to it (low status). Next we see the hands behind the head opening themselves up, giving an outward focus and so indicating vulnerability (High status). Casting our eyes downward we see the legs are crossed thus closing themselves off with barriers (Low status). Generally this position is quite an arrogant one, the top half tends to indicate insecurity within the person and has an open, but unsure, 'feel' to it, while the legs are crossed, protecting this insecurity.

This position would indicate to me that they 'think' they know what they are talking about but are not open to any ideas to the contrary.

In any evaluation for the purpose of study or preparation, isolating the various parts of the body and viewing each in light of vulnerabilities etc, will give a fairly accurate account of status, with an insight to the underlying emotional state. Please remember that it is very important to take the position studied, if in 'real' life, within its context. For example the man leaning to one side could be doing so because he has only one leg! Likewise the woman with her arms crossed may be in sub zero temperature.

Even though the environment, or a physical impairment, may be the initial driver behind some body language, the position adopted will in turn effect the person's emotional state.

So, not only does the way a person feel become reflected in their bodies, but also the way their bodies and weight is carried will effect how they feel. If you start walking around with your physical body reflecting low status, then you will most likely find yourself feeling low status, and likewise if you walk around posturing a high status, then this in turn will make you feel high status, or powerful and in control. Walking with shifting weight will soon have you feeling indecisive; constantly evaluating.

Try walking around with your chest out, head high, body centered and focus outward. This position will rapidly give you a 'superior' feeling (High status).

And if you walk with your head down, off center and focus inward, this will give you an inferior feel (Low status).

**Try them!**

People habitually try to make themselves comfortable. When asking some students why they lean to the side and fold their arms when they stand, they reply;

**"No reason, it's just comfortable, I always stand like this".**

What we must look at is why it is comfortable and, if they always stand that way, what does it tell you about them. The position will be comfortable because it reinforces the way they feel. If you put them into a technically more relaxed position they reply that it is uncomfortable, this being because their external does not now adequately reflect their feelings. If the person 'opens' themselves to their new position, be it relaxed, uncomfortable or otherwise, they will soon start to be effected by the position and thus their feelings will move in the direction of harmony with their physical body.

This manipulation of weight distribution is very useful in character preparation; you've probably already realized some of the possibilities. We will be talking more about this in a later Chapter.

What happens when we try to cover our feelings using our external? You will remember from Chapter 2 that when an emotion is re-labelled the primary emotion manifests somewhere in the body. When looking at status these manifestations can have a big influence.

**For example;**

Tanya and Rhonda are having an argument that looks like it may turn to physical violence. Tanya's initial Emotion is fear but she doesn't want to show that fear and so tries to appear calm and confident by standing Centred with her arms by her sides.

Unfortunately for Tanya the attempted suppression of the Initial Emotion manifests into her hands, and so even though they are by her sides;

**Open, Vulnerable and High Status.**

They are visibly shaking;

**Shifting Weight, Evaluation, Low Status**

The covering up or re-labelling of the Initial Emotion may manifest in numerous different ways;

Ie, sweating, shaking, choked up throat, and in extreme situations wetting yourself!

Probably the most salient occurrence for actors of an attempted cover up is seen in 'Stage fright'. The actor goes onto stage with a Primary Emotion of fear; tries to look calm, all the while their hands are shaking vigorously. If this fear is adequately consciously relabelled however, rather than covered over, then stage fright can not only be eliminated, but can be used to drive the emotional preparation for the performance. More on this in Chapter Seven.

So far we have looked at Interactional status, this is the status that is born from the unique current interaction. We'll take a quick look at the other type of status which is called 'Social Status', a term you've probably come across before.

## Social Status

'Social Status' is the assumed status given to a social position due to its perceived importance within a society.

In life we often hear catch-phrases like;

'Climbing up the corporate ladder'
'Moving up in the world'
'Reaching new heights'
'Aiming for the stars'
'Playing with the big boys'
'Upper Class'
'Middle Class'
'Sinking to new lows'
'In the pits'
'Lower Class'

All these phrases are referring to a relative perceived social status. If you are 'Climbing the corporate ladder', then this means that you are gaining status in the corporate world. The notion of height and moving upward is a characteristic of high or gaining high, status.

This reference to levels of height can be seen throughout our perceived social status vocabulary. Have a look back at the examples and note all the references to height, or relative height.

As mentioned earlier in this Chapter the terms we use for individuals in these positions of social status also reflect status levels.

The Headmaster in a school is another example. Head refers to the top of an organization, originally derived from your head being the upper part of your body. So we see the '**Head**master' being higher in status than the 'Student ***Body***'.

'High Priest' in a religious organization. Again we see this height referring to their status within the organization.

There are many other examples, take some time to think about what other areas of life have references to status within their terms.

Within organizations there are hierarchical structures of status. Here are a few examples, left to right, of relative statuses within social structures starting with the highest first. Note, not all levels are shown.

**Highest                          to                          Lowest**

| Pilot | Co-Pilot | Steward |
| --- | --- | --- |
| General | Major | Private |
| Principal | Vice-Principal | Teacher |
| CEO | Manager | Employee |
| Queen | Princess | Duchess |
| Pope | Priest | Clergy |
| Captain | Vice-Captain | Prefect |
| Captain | First Officer | Deckhand |

It is quite common for comedy to be based around a discrepancy between the Social Status and the Interactional Status.

For example, you may have a situation in an army genre where a Captain has a higher interactional status than a Major. This is regularly the case in the old television comedy M.A.S.H. Often Captain Hawkeye Pearce is higher in interactional status than Major Frank Burns.

In the second series of 'Black Adder', Edmond is quite often higher in status than the Prince.

Throughout the history of Theatre, Television and Film there are numerous instances where the 'slave' has a higher interactional status than the 'master'. Commedia-Del-Arte often used this discrepancy between the Interactional Status and the Social Status for great comic effect.

For the most part, as an actor, you will be concerned with Interactional Status. Even though there may be a discrepancy between your character's Social Status and their Interactional Status, in the enactment it is being connected to the 'Other' that you need to be concerned with. The audience will view the discrepancy within the scene.

### *Practical Exercises*

1) Go and hire or buy the film **'Crimson Tide'** watch it closely for the status interactions, make notes on your observations.

2) Observe your own Vulnerabilities and barriers in action and watch those of others.

3) Try manipulating your vulnerabilities by allowing yourself to be vulnerable in situations where you would usually put up a barrier. How does this make you feel? Be consciously aware of any salient sensations or emotions.

4) Watch closely the status interactions in your life. How are the interactions different from school or work? How are they the same? Who are the people that raise you in status and who lowers you? Who do you raise in status and whom do you lower?

5) Observe in the environment the physicalities of status: Office furniture arrangement, bus seating, theatre seating, airport fixtures, colors, fonts used, uniforms, basically look at physical things which give a person or environment high or low status.

# CHAPTER 5

# *Personal Space & Focus*

## The Comfort Zone

## Personal Space

Personal space is a concept that is not often adequately defined. Because Personal Space changes in every individual situation, coming up with a general definition is not easy.

The definition of the 'normal' area of personal space for an individual, that is, the initial personal space at the beginning of an interaction, we will define as;

**"The comfortable distance of interaction with any individual, group of individuals, animal, environment, object, item or stimuli, in a specific situation, before tertiary cognition, in the first Interaction."**

First up let's have a look at our definition and break it up into digestible pieces.

'**The comfortable distance of interaction...**'

This is fairly self-explanatory. This relates to the distance between yourself and the 'Other' that you find comfortable for interaction.

So what are your 'Others'?

'...**Any individual, group of individuals, animal, environment, object, item or stimuli**...'

These 'Others' are simply those things that may have an effect on you. Stimuli, in this instance, pertains to any incoming information, ie, sights, sounds, smells, tastes, physical sensations.

'...**in a specific situation**...'

All situations are different. At the time of interaction we are interested in the uniqueness of the moment. We may react differently to the same stimuli in different situations and thus field different areas of Personal Space. Ie; you may react differently to seeing your boss at work as opposed to the pub. A surgeon may react differently to seeing her dog at home as opposed to in the operating theatre. And so it is important to recognize that the specifics of the situation have a big impact on your initial reactions. The antecedent cue, in operant conditioning, sees the setting of the scene for particular Behaviours or reactions to take place. The next part of the definition;

### 'before tertiary cognition...'

The reason we define 'normal' Personal Space before entering Tertiary Cognition is because after we have worked on the incoming information to a greater depth our focus for the barrier changes. For example;

You are at a party and you see a friend that you haven't seen for a few months. In the Need stage you want to make contact with them, this pushes your Personal Space out. However, upon entering the Evaluation Stage you remember that you still owe them one hundred dollars. Your personal space shrinks as you try to make your way out of the back door without being seen.

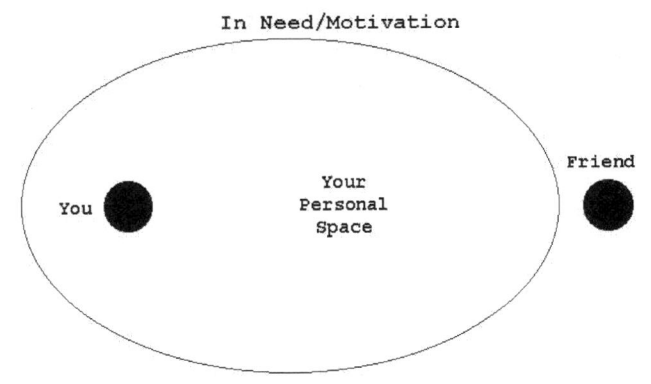

In Need/Motivation

You — Your Personal Space — Friend

```
             In Evaluation
        Your
      Personal
       Space

    ⬇
  ┌─────┐              ┌────────┐
  │You ● │              │Friend ●│
  └─────┘              └────────┘
```

If in the Evaluation Stage you had remembered that this friend actually owes you one hundred dollars, then your Personal Space may look something like this;

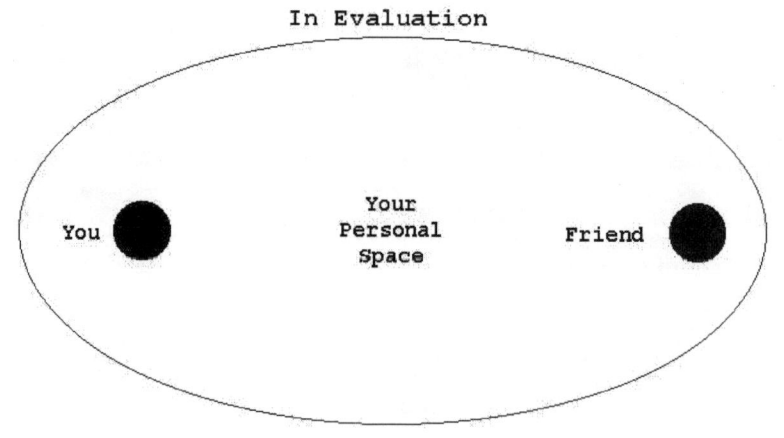

```
             In Evaluation

   ╭─────────────────────────────────────╮
   │                 Your                 │
   │  You ●       Personal      Friend ● │
   │                Space                 │
   ╰─────────────────────────────────────╯
```

...as you make your way over to them! Back to the final part of our definition.

### '...in the first Interaction.'

The reason that we are defining the 'normal' Personal Space during the first interaction is because of the changes that occur after that. The first interaction gives us a reference point when looking at characters and how they are affecting, or being effected by their environment. When talking, or thinking about Personal Space it helps for you to be able to make decisions about how that space is manipulated after that first interaction.

Without this part of the definition we would be in a constant state of redefining our 'normal' personal space and this is just not practical for our purposes.

For instance in the example where your friend owes you one hundred dollars, the next interaction that you go through as you are making your way towards them, sees you already with your Personal Space over the top of them. If we now define that as 'normal' then we start tripping over the different *'normals'*, when talking about it. This will make more sense as we progress.

## What makes up our Personal Space?

Personal space holds within it the **vulnerabilities** that the outer edge **barriers** protect.

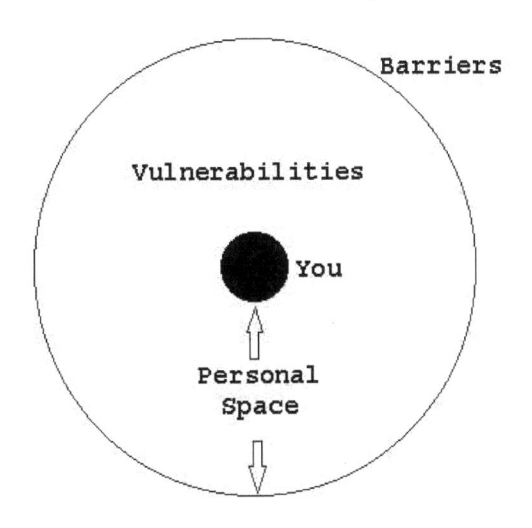

```
                                    Barriers
                    Vulnerabilities
                          You
                          ⇧
                      Personal
                       Space
                          ⇩
```

The vulnerabilities inside our Personal Space, as previously discussed, and the subsequent protective barrier, consist of;

**Intellectual** ⇐-------------⇒ **Emotional**

**Social** ⇐------------⇒ **Personal**

So, if your character is Emotionally/Socially Vulnerable, then their Personal Space will see an Intellectual/Personal Barrier, protecting their Emotional/Social Vulnerabilities. (See Chapter Four)

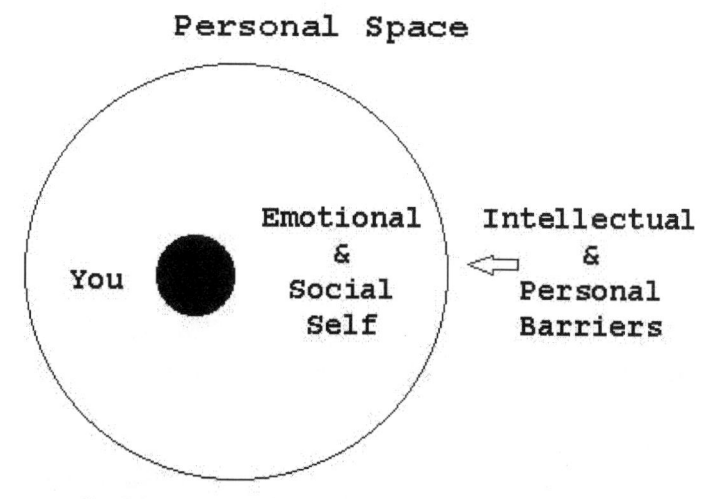

**Personal Space**

You — Emotional & Social Self ⇐ Intellectual & Personal Barriers

## *Personal Space Origins*

Personal Space is a product of an individuals previous, current and possible future environments. Each individual has a preferred area of 'Normal' interaction due to their past environments and experience. This utilisation of past experience is then used in assessing the current situational interaction and modified accordingly.

Future awareness also effects the current state of Personal Space and focus. For example;

Herman is at a party chatting up Rhonda, the girl of his dreams. Herman's knowledge that Tony, Rhonda's brother and martial arts expert, could arrive at any moment will have a large influence on Herman's area of focus and current personal space. Would you like to be caught in a close Personal Space interaction with the little sister of a killing machine? And so, as we observed in Operant Conditioning, the antecedent cue of talking to Rhonda, sets the scene for a possible confrontation with Tony. This *possibility* effects Herman's Personal Space.

Personal space differs greatly between people of differing background environments. For example people raised in the country generally have a different personal space, or interaction area, than those brought up in the inner city. The environment and its limitations or characteristics will influence the comfortable interaction zones of those who resided in them.

## Country

Firstly, let's look at those people brought up in the country.

What limitations, characteristics and influences does a country environment have? The country is characterised by **wide open spaces**, with neighbours often being kilometres away. There is **very little noise** in the country and sounds can travel some distance. When looking out over a vast landscape with no people in sight, we have no need to hold up barriers in front of ourselves because there is no one to defend against. And so we can open ourselves up, becoming very vulnerable thus giving us a high status and a feeling of power and control. Because there is no one in perception, in this given situation, the environment actually allows us to push our personal space far out over the land.

If you have ever stood on a cliff and looked out over the ocean, or on a mountain looking over country plains, then you will be familiar with the relaxing, powerful feeling that accompanies it. This feeling is due to the expansion of your Personal Space, which in effect means that you 'own' or 'command' the area you are viewing since you have become totally vulnerable to it. You may have heard the phrase 'taking in the view'. This feeling of 'taking in', is due to you taking the environment into your own personal space.

If someone suddenly appeared in your view, generally speaking your personal space would immediately shrink to keep the 'intruder' out. You now have to share the area with someone else and so it loses much of its appeal due to the shrinking of your Personal Space and the barriers that have to be put up to accommodate the intruder.

Now let's look at what effect this has on people constantly in this environment. If they are constantly letting their personal spaces reach out over vast distances, then, in an interaction it would be reasonable to assume that they would feel more comfortable with a 'largish' 'normal' Personal Space.

Another environmental factor is the amount of background noise. Since it is generally fairly quiet in the country, there is no need for them to raise their voices to be heard, and so conversing at a distance, ie 3-4 meters, is possible without any strain. With all this in mind it is reasonable to assume that country folk would generally prefer a relatively large 'normal' area of Personal Space.

When viewing these country residents this can be seen to be true. Even when people brought up in the country shake hands, they tend to stop out of reach of the other person and lean inward to accept the handshake.

## City

Lets now turn our attention to the other end of the scale and view the inner city environment. The inner city environment is characterised by **tight spaces**, small enclosures and limited 'line-of-sight'. In fact, the environment is very closed-in with little room for personal space expansion. Neighbours are often only a few feet away through a wall, compared to the kilometres in the country.

**Noise pollution** in the city is high with traffic, building sites, police and ambulance sirens, people walking past, aeroplanes and the stereo down the road, all competing for attention. With noise making it possible to be heard only at short distances and the closed in spaces of the city, personal space is drawn inwards and so interaction is at a closer range.

All these factors see people living in our cities preferring a relatively small 'normal' Personal Space. People talk at a shorter distance, they shake hands at a closer range, they generally feel comfortable interacting closer than their country counterparts.

Most people lie somewhere on the continuum from a totally enclosed environment to a totally open one, and so their personal space will be affected accordingly.

**What does this mean for the actor?**

A characters' Personal Space will have an effect on the performance interaction. For example, you're in a film where you play Bob, the highflying executive who was born and raised in the inner city environment. You are in your penthouse office when Luke, the born and bred farmer from outback Australia, confronts you.

Luke and his new wife, Jessie-May, have entered your office and are livid about your company's proposed nuclear waste storage facility that will be constructed next to their Pig Farm, the local preschool, The Blessed Augusta Nursing home and the 'Beaut Outback Mineral Water' bottling spring.

We shall define the players' vulnerabilities as follows;

**BOB**
*Emotionally/Socially Vulnerable*

**LUKE**
*Intellectually/Personally Vulnerable*

**JESSIE-MAY**
*Intellectually/Socially Vulnerable*

Luke enters, he is emotionally charged as he confronts Bob. Jessie-May is also emotional and stays close to Luke,(Socially Vulnerable) Bob keeps his emotions in check, opting for an intellectual stance.

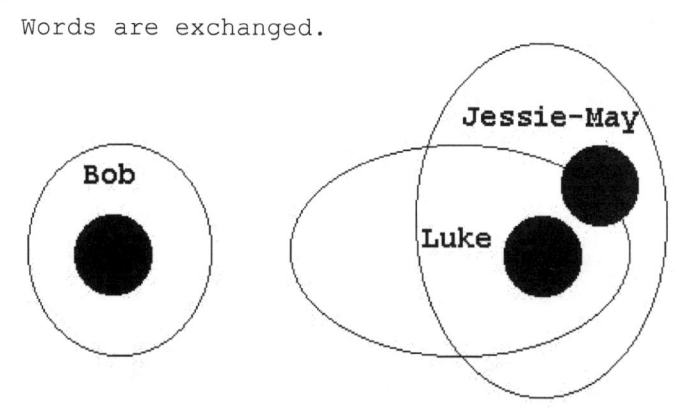

Words are exchanged.

As the confrontation proceeds Bob approaches Luke, trying to reason with him. Jessie-May shrinks her personal space as Bob approaches. For this example Bob and Luke maintain their preferred normal Personal Spaces. Because Luke's normal Personal Space is larger than Bob's, Bob invades Lukes' Personal Space before Luke invades Bob's.

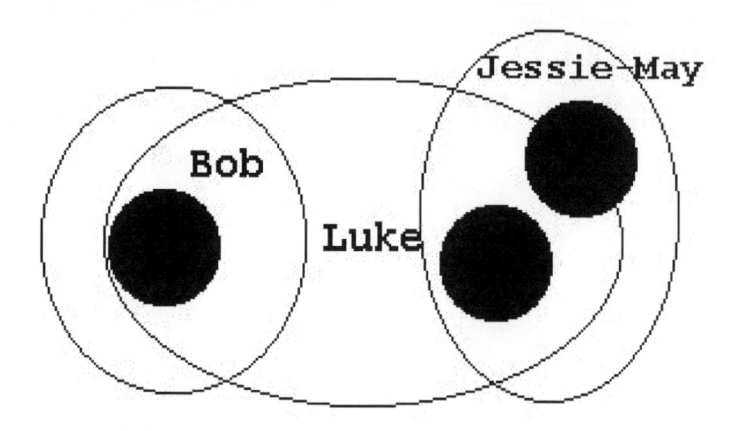

Luke is now in a situation where he either;
1   Backs off to maintain his Personal Space.
2   Calls on his full barrier to protect his Personal Space, that is, maybe he physically attacks Bob.

3 Defends on his vulnerable side and starts trying to reason with Bob.
4 Allows himself to become vulnerable, letting Bob enter his Personal Space.

Remember, Bob is still feeling quite safe at this distance. For argument's sake let's assume that Luke proceeds to physically attack Bob. What does Bob do?

Luke has now broken through Bob's Personal Space barriers, forcing Bob to interact with his vulnerable side as well. Jessie-May has left the office to get some-one to break them up.

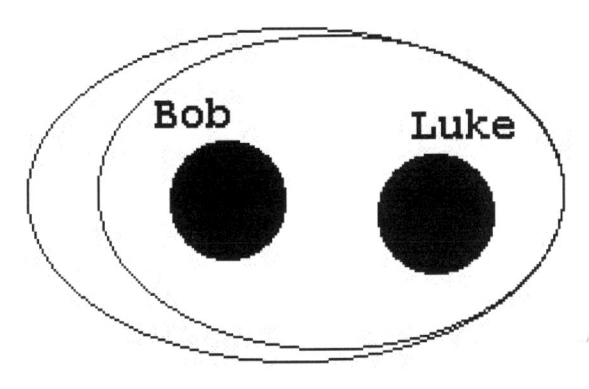

Bob now starts to fight back while calling for help. As an actor playing Bob, you know that you can get close to Luke before feeling threatened. Playing Luke sees you wanting to keep a slightly greater distance away.

Now this could have been slightly different if Luke had entered the room not only emotional but also looking physically violent and pushing his personal space out further in front of him. This being the case he may have broken through Bob's Intellectual barrier very early; Bob's thinking going something like,

**"This guy is going to kill me, I cannot reason with him!"**

And so Bob may have called for help immediately, or maybe even pulled a gun out of his top drawer.

**All as a result of the 'Other'.**

Even in general conversation, if a city person and a country person are interacting, the country person may feel ill at ease if the city person tries to converse at their normal interaction distance. The country person's Personal Space sees them uncomfortable interacting at a close range.

You may recall moments in your own life when you have been talking with someone who comes very close to you, making you feel uncomfortable. One particular Seinfeld Episode saw a character who had a very small personal space, try to interact at a very close range thus forcing people back as they in turn tried to get to a comfortable distance of interaction for themselves.

The next time you are out talking with people, try moving in a little closer than normal. You will probably feel a bit uneasy as they are now inside your own Personal Space. You most likely won't have to wait long before they subtly move back to allow themselves a more comfortable interaction distance.

Likewise, you may want to try staying a bit further away than usual and watch people move closer. As they move closer, you move back a bit. If they notice your uneasiness at the closer interaction they will probably allow you that distance, after all, you are not intruding on their Personal Space.

It is helpful for you to know your 'characters' interaction distance, which will be explored during the actors character background preparation. (Background preparation shall be dealt with in a later Chapter).

## *Manipulating Personal Space*

Personal Space can manipulated to effect the other person, it can be enlarged or withdrawn using the concept of focus.

A country landscape, without wildlife, is generally not a 'busy' scene; it can be viewed with a single perception because there is no one in it to draw our attention. This landscape does not have many distractions or items that require great attention to view.

On the other hand, for example, a dance party is a 'busy' scene with a crowded floor offering a great deal of ever changing things on which you can focus or give attention to.

Usually in this situation attention is split between a variety of things. For example, at the dance party you may be listening to the song that is playing, dancing, trying to impress your date, looking to see how your friend is going, keeping away from a jerk that you find really annoying, trying not to spill your drink on the radical 'Disco King' next to you and making sure that the bouncer doesn't see you dancing with a drink in your hand.

All of this adds up to dispersed attention and a personal space that is very shallow due to defending against so many possible intrusions. What happens now if we try to manipulate our personal space through focus?

*Focus*

We will look at two different kinds of focus;

## Cognitive Focus

**The measure of cognitive attention given to a need.**

## Physical Focus

**The degree to which the physical directs attention.**

With the Dance Party environment example, from the myriad of stimuli and 'Others' that we may wish to address, let's restrict ourselves to only one point of focus, the jerk on the other side of the dance floor that annoys you.

And further, we shall focus on only one course of action, or need, associated with this person and that is, to kill them.

Because we don't care about anything else in the room, we don't defend against it and so we are vulnerable to them. Our Personal Space is now enlarged so as to include the jerk over at the other side of the room because we want to effect them. This focus on effecting the other person, ie, killing, to the exclusion of all other possible focuses will force out our Personal Space and most likely move whoever is in the path of focus aside. (This being because we have also encroached on their Personal Spaces as well)

If you're game, test this one out the next time you are at a dance party, put your full and total focus on an imaginary person at the other side of the room and focus on killing them. Remember TOTAL focus is required. Now start to advance towards them slowly. Everyone in the path you are walking will quickly get out of the way. The focus is pushing out your personal space. You'll notice that as you are walking with focus your body weight will be down and Centred as is seen in the Realization/acceptance stage of interaction.

Once you have done this try the same thing again, this time don't focus, just walk across the room to a random point, you will notice a big difference.

On the other side of the coin, we can also shrink our personal space to encompass only ourselves. We know that the environment that causes a small normal Personal Space is an enclosed environment with very little room for personal space expansion, as is found in an inner city region. To bring our Personal Space to encompass only our body requires focus inwardly or on our own external.

A very self-conscious person who constantly focuses on him or herself would have a very small Personal Space. A person who has just been attacked, might retreat to a corner and make him or herself into as small a ball as possible. This withdrawal into themselves and into a ball is so that the area they have to protect is as small as can be.

In 'normal' interaction only a limited amount of protection is necessary, however, in an abnormal situation it may be necessary to retreat and put up barriers closer to ourselves.

You can see this same principal in the military. If an area is under attack and is likely to fall, then a common strategy is to withdraw to protect a smaller front. It stands to reason that it is easier for one thousand soldiers to guard one fort than it is for the same thousand to guard the entire Australian coastline.

This same principle works with people. If under a sufficiently harmful attack, they may withdraw their personal space to include only their bodies. Some extreme cases have been noted of soldiers who have been tortured severely and survived. It has been related in a number of instances that the soldiers have sought refuge within their imagination and away from the torture inflicted on their physical bodies. This is an example of where someone has withdrawn their personal space further than their own physical bodies, so as to allow protection only for their consciousness.

As the imagination is the last barrier, once this has been destroyed the person has been 'broken'. This person no longer holds any value on any aspect of their individuality and thus cannot be 'effected'.

## Proximetrics

Proximetrics refers to the relative physical proximity of one 'Other' to another 'Other'.

When one character is higher than another, purely by physical relationship, the higher character has the higher status. This is because on a physical level the Personal Space of the higher character goes over the top of the relatively lower character, thus making them vulnerable, thus raising their status.

Quite often in institutional environments there are physical differences between 'Others' to give a higher or lower status.

In a courtroom the judge is nearly always seated higher than the rest of the court. This physicality of Proximetrics raises them in the Interactional Status, aided by their perceived Social Status.

Some corporate executives will have their desk slightly raised within their office to raise them in status.

In the theatre, balcony seats are traditionally the domain of the upper-class.

As mentioned earlier the Proximetrics of Adolf Hitler when addressing the people meant that his status was raised.

In the film industry short actors who are in leading roles are often shot from an angle looking slightly up at them. This is to raise their status. It is not uncommon for a short leading actor to have other short actors cast around them to facilitate this status.

That is all for Proximetrics for now, it is generally the domain for the Director, D.O.P. and other production roles to sort out but is important for you to be aware of it. Where you are placed on the stage in relation to the other cast, or what angle you are shot from in a film, may have a significant effect on the audience's perception of your character.

## The Seven Areas of Personal Space

We will look at dividing Personal Space up into seven major categories. These categories consist of areas of focus, which contain within them, Personal Space. The focus barriers start with number one being our closest or smallest area of Personal Space and extend out to number seven which is our furthest or largest area of Personal Space.

## 1) *Withdrawn Imagination*

When an individuals protective barrier is focused and contained within the imagination at the *exclusion* of any external reality.

The first category is called 'Withdrawn Imagination'. This is when a person no longer protects their body and so puts up their barriers within their imagination. Imaginational barriers include imagining being somewhere else, totally ignoring any physical attack or confrontation. Rape is another possible event where this area of focus could be utilised. A person being raped may choose to imagine being somewhere else, rather than face up to their physical reality.

If a person cannot totally shut off their physical reality, they may also change it using their imagination, to make it more acceptable.

For example, Rhonda, our neurotic teenager, is at a party where every boy that she likes has been paired off with someone. Rhonda 'needs' some male company and so scans the remaining boys. Myron, a short, pale and slightly gross boy would like some female company. Rhonda and Myron's eyes meet and they start talking. One thing leads to another and the two start kissing.

All is good in Myron's world. However, Rhonda is having trouble kissing a guy who she thinks has as much personality as a house brick and so resorts to her imagination. Rhonda now imagines that she is actually kissing Andrew, the star of the schools football team, and so she has mixed her 'Withdrawn Imagination', with her physical reality.

Withdrawn Imagination also happens quite often in everyday life. Let's say that you are in a crowded elevator. Because of the size of the elevator people are in contact with you from all sides. What do you do in this situation? Most people go into their imagination. They may look up at the level numbers (giving their personal space room) while thinking about where they are going or what they have to do today. Basically they take their mind off their current physicality and find comfort within their imaginations or mind.

## 2) Physical Body

When an individuals protective barrier is focused on their physical body or an extension thereof.

The second area is that encompassing the 'Physical Body'. This area will see the person involved concentrating their focus onto themselves or extensions of themselves. Some examples include;

Cleaning fingernails, examining a cut, squeezing a pimple, brushing down pants and washing hands. These are all focusing on your own 'Physical Body'

This area also includes the protection of the physical body. That is stopping, or trying to stop, some one or something from touching your physical body, or removing something that is connected with your body.

In an interaction with a person this may be seen when warding off someone who is trying to touch you. If you have ever felt that you don't want another person to touch you then you have, at that moment, withdrawn your personal space to include only your physical body.

Have you ever been on a bus or train and had someone that you didn't know come and sit down next to you? Because of the restricted nature of seating there was a possibility that your bodies would be touching. Ever felt that awkward feeling as you realize your leg is touching the person next to you? And you try, so subtly to inch your leg away so that contact is not made. This is protecting at the Physical Body Level.

Maybe you found the person who sat next to you physically attractive. Maybe you enjoyed the touching of legs. Maybe they were subtly trying to inch away from you!

So what happened when you were on the bus or train and you wanted to protect at the Physical Body level but couldn't? There wasn't enough room so your legs had to touch. Maybe you changed seats, maybe you just stood up, or maybe you looked out of the window and went into Withdrawn Imagination...

Touch is a very personal thing and if people that we like and/or respect physically touch us, then this usually results in a lifting of confidence and a 'warm', 'safe' feeling inside.

Touch is a very powerful tool for actors; it can be used in many different ways. Touch can see a loving bond reinforced or a death threat consummated. Every time we touch a powerful statement is made so be aware, as an actor, what statement you are making.

## 3) *Shallow*

When an individual's protective barrier is focused and contained within an area around them which seeks an interaction at a distance that maintains their barriers so as not to connect with the barriers of others.

The third area of focus for Personal Space is 'Shallow', this is when we withdraw our personal space closer to our bodies than in a 'normal' interaction. This is often done when there are a number of people around, in a crowd, at a party, in a cue etc. The are numerous other times when our Personal Space is 'Shallow'. We shall look at a few.

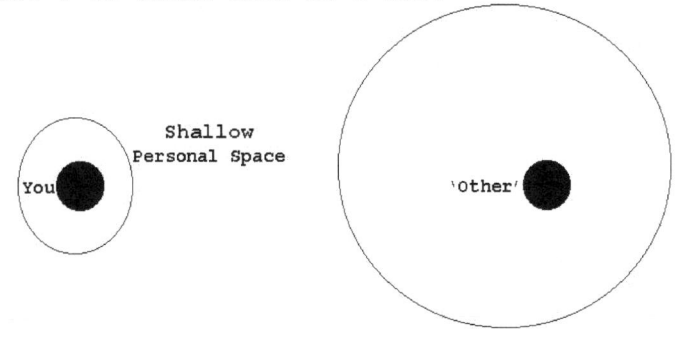

Herman, our intrepid hero, is at a party enjoying himself chatting up Rhonda when suddenly he sees Tony, our ruthless barbarian Ninja and brother of Rhonda walk in. After 'realising' that it is Tony and the implications therein, Herman doesn't want to be seen in such close proximity with his sister and so consequently withdraws his focus and personal space to shallower than 'normal'. Herman is not successful for long, Tony spies him with his little sister and so makes his way towards them. Tony's Personal Space extends. Herman isn't inclined to partake in small talk with Tony and so takes himself and his Personal Space out the back door.

Cast your mind back to when you were at school, or maybe you're still there. If you ever received or witnessed someone receiving a scolding from a teacher you may have noticed yourself, or the third party, retreat to a shallow area of Personal Space. Head bowed down, inward focus... not daring to move their Personal Space outward by looking the teacher in the eye.

Shy people tend to stay in a 'Shallow' area of Personal Space. If you've seen someone who is very shy often you'll notice their focus is close to their body rather than extended outward.

Dustin Hoffman, who played 'Raymond' in, 'Rain Man', tended to stay in a Shallow area of Personal Space. As mentioned in the second Chapter, 'Raymond' also spent most of his time within the 'Evaluation' stage of the interaction. So, when approaching a character like 'Raymond', we can see that knowing he is constantly trying to 'work-things-out' and has an inward focus can lead us to finding answers within the Evaluation and in Personal Space. 'Raymond' was constantly shifting in weight and had an inward focus.

From this information we can glean that he is generally low status and Emotionally/Socially Vulnerable. Low status because of the close barrier and shifting of weight signifying evaluation, and Emotionally/Socially vulnerable because;

1) He is constantly thinking and so that is his main Personal Barrier, and;

2) Socially vulnerable because of his withdrawn Personal Space in 'Shallow', thus trying to shut out social interactions.

## 4) Normal

When an individuals protective barrier is focused at a comfortable distance so as to maintain a non-threatening interaction.

The forth category is called Normal. It is that base or 'normal' area of interaction as defined at the beginning of this Chapter.

**"The comfortable distance of interaction with any individual, group of individuals, animal, environment, object, item or stimuli, in a specific situation, before tertiary cognition in the first Interaction."**

It is also the area we generally spend most our time in. When you are talking with friends in a relaxed general way, you are, for the most part in Normal Personal Space. This may change if the conversation starts getting intensive, ie, your Personal Space may extend, or if you are insulted or embarrassed in some way your Personal Space may shrink to Shallow.

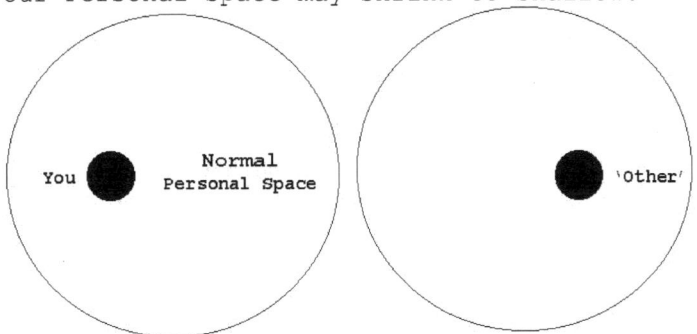

You ●    Normal Personal Space      ● 'Other'

Even though the definition may sound very technical, don't worry too much about it, it is that area you feel comfortable in when talking with friends.

*Robert Carne*
## 5) **Deep**

When an individual's protective barrier is focused and contained to the inclusion of an other, the `other' becomes inside the individuals Personal Space.

The fifth area of Personal Space is that of 'Deep'. This occurs when we extend our normal personal space outwards to include one 'Other' or one chunk of 'Others'. The focus is now further than normal interaction, ie, watching someone dancing, a show, spying on someone etc. In this area you are extending your personal space to encompass that which you would not have under 'normal' circumstances, in fact you are becoming vulnerable to the target of your focus.

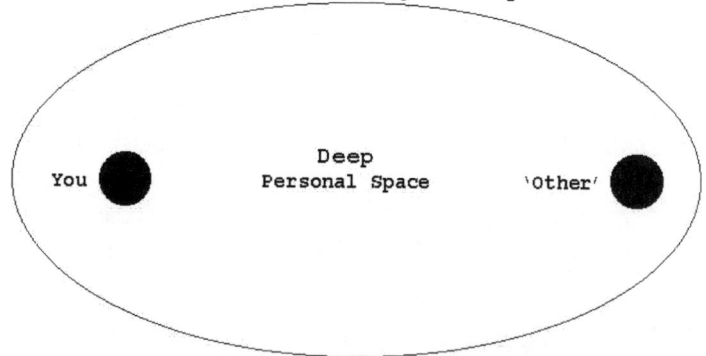

```
         Deep
You    Personal Space    'Other'
```

It is in the area of 'Deep' that you start to rise in status as your Personal space encompasses the 'Other'.

The pushing out of your Personal Space into the 'Deep' area is achieved by concentrating your cognitive focus on one 'Other' or one chunk. If you are involved in a "Deep & Meaningful" conversation then the concentrated focus sees you going into the Deep area of Personal Space.

Again think back to your school days and the teacher who was scolding the student. While the student may have been withdrawing their Personal Space to 'Shallow' the teacher was expanding their Personal Space to that of 'Deep'.

You may at some stage have seen a friend who was obviously distressed because it was written all over their face. As you asked, "What's wrong?" your Personal Space moved out into 'Deep' as you tried to study their face to work out what the problem was.

Whenever you allow one 'Other', or one chunk, into your Personal Space, ie, become vulnerable to it, then you are in the area of 'Deep' Personal Space.

## 6) Infinite Reality

When an individual's protective barrier is focused and contained within an area that encompasses all that is within sensual reality.

The sixth area of personal space is called 'Infinite Reality'. This is when we extend our personal space out as far as we can see or perceive with one of our main five senses.

For example, imagine that you are standing on a high cliff top looking out over the ocean. There are no people only water and sky as far as the eye can see. Your Personal Space reaches out covering the entire perceptual range. The feeling you have is one of power as you take command of all that you view. You are vulnerable to the entire scene elevating your status and giving you a feeling of power. As a good friend of mine, Anthony Bova, once told me,

"You don't walk five thousand miles to speak with the Guru at the **bottom** of the mountain!"

Now imagine yourself standing on a cliff overlooking a vast valley. Your personal space reaches out. Now imagine that there is no-one for a hundred kilometres, you stand there in the morning light, totally naked, totally vulnerable. Close you eyes now and picture that, then open them and read on.

Now, as you stand there, your Personal Space commanding everything you view, something catches your eye. You look across the mountain to see a troupe of boy scouts coming up a path towards you. Your Personal

Space snaps back, you withdraw into 'Shallow' as you run back to your hut for clothes! (Except for all you sicko's out there who stand your ground and start performing a rain dance!)

If you have ever seen any footage of Adolf Hitler addressing masses of people from his podium, his position is elevated, his arms are open, his personal space covers all that are present. His physicality and vulnerability give him a huge elevation in status.

You may have watched a live theatre performance where one of the characters has showed amazing stage presence. Most of the time you are witnessing someone who can control their Personal Space, consciously or not, so as to allow the entire audience into their space. This vulnerability to the audience has tremendous power for the actor. Most truly great actors can become vulnerable to an audience, or camera, at will. These actors can take the audience with them on their journey as they allow their viewers into their own Personal Space.

Don't take this information lightly; being able to become truly vulnerable to an entire audience is one of the most powerful skills you can learn. You'll need to be operating so that the audience can see your initial emotion **and** see that you are maintaining, or trying to maintain an effective emotional barrier. **And then** let them watch that barrier dissolve. Letting go of all your barriers and allowing the world to see you as you truly are can be very scary!

In the `Infinite Reality' area of Personal Space the only perimeter is that of reality. When viewing the stars we are allowing our personal space out as far as the eyes can see, as far as our reality allows.

## 7) Expanded Imagination

When an individual's protective barrier is focused and contained within the imagination and with the *inclusion* of all external reality.

The seventh and final area of Personal Space is that of 'Expanded Imagination'. 'Expanded Imagination' is when our focus and Personal Space extends to further than we can see or perceive with our senses.

For example, looking up at the night sky, pondering the universe and wondering about life on other planets. Note that this differs from 'Infinite Reality' in that the imagination or 'non-reality' is brought into play.

Most forms of daydreaming would come in this category, as would many forms of a drug-induced state.

Expanded Imagination allows for the Personal Space to 'take-for-granted' our current reality, accept it, put it consciously to one side while allowing in the infinite possibilities that our imagination may conjure.

**Final Words**

We have discussed that personal space is an area that determines our comfortable interaction space. To encroach on someone's personal space is to go through his or her barriers.

A person who can manipulate and control their Personal Space and Status can defend how they want to, or not at all. This person shows good control over situations and can elicit almost any response. Good 'power-players' are generally good at status manipulation. Remember, the more vulnerable and the less 'need', the higher the status, and, the less vulnerable and the more 'need', the lower the status.

All of these areas of Personal Space and the focus involved can be used in conjunction with the `Interaction Model' and Vulnerability traits, to greatly enhance the preparation stage of Acting. There can be some very interesting comedic situations to be found in seeing two people supposedly 'interacting', but in different areas of Personal Space.

## Seven Areas of Personal Space

1) **Withdrawn Imagination**
   When an individual's protective barrier is focused and contained within the imagination at the *exclusion* of any external reality.

2) **Physical Body**
   When an individual's protective barrier is focused on their physical body or an extension thereof.

3) **Shallow**
   When an individual's protective barrier is focused and contained within an area around them which seeks an interaction at a distance that maintains their barriers so as not to connect with the barriers of others.

4) **Normal**
   When an individual's protective barrier is focused at a comfortable distance so as to maintain a non-threatening interaction.

5) **Deep**
   When an individual's protective barrier is focused and contained to the inclusion of an 'other', the 'other' becomes inside the individual's Personal Space.

6) **Infinite Reality**
   When an individual's protective barrier is focused and contained within an area that encompasses all that is within sensual reality.

7) **Expanded Imagination**
   When an individual's protective barrier is focused and contained within the imagination and with the *inclusion* of all external reality.

## Practical Exercises

How large do you think your 'Normal' Personal Space is? Start to be aware of your own Personal Space and how you use it. Try some social experiments. Sit next to someone on an otherwise empty bus; Talk at a closer, or greater distance than you usually would. See what happens.

Manipulate your focus in social situations to change your Personal Space. The next time an attractive person looks at you, do you look away and withdraw your Personal Space, or do you hold eye contact and increase your Personal Space? Try both see what happens.

If you haven't already you should be trying to incorporate all you have learnt into your acting. Test things out in the classroom, or for those brave souls, on the stage. By now, if you are actively involved with classes or productions, you should be working the theoretical into practical application.

Watch other people's Personal Spaces and see the interactions involved. Night clubs or dances are great places to watch Personal Space. Most body language is Personal Space adjustments. A guy goes to ask a girl to dance, watch his and her Personal Space. Is he confident (Deep) or unconfident (Shallow), Is she interested (Deep) or repulsed (Physical Body). If he is rejected where does his Personal Space go? Shallow? Deep?

Watch groups on the dance floor. Who is interested in who? What do their Personal Spaces tell you?

Have fun, watch closely the interactions in every day life.

**CHAPTER 6**

## *Memory, Behaviour and the Script*

```
Ummm ..... Line?!
```

# Memory

Knowledge of memory and how we remember is another important element of acting. If a scene entails a character to recall events of the past then how they go about it can be important. Likewise, if suddenly a character remembers something, the actor may want to know what the cues that brought about them remembering it were.

One of the most important, and often overlooked, components of acting is the way that the actor memorizes their lines. Line memorizing can play a huge role in the ultimate delivery of dialogue, get that wrong and everything else can follow suit.

To start with we shall look at memory in general, in particular at the initial encoding of information into memory.

## *Encoding Specificity*

Information is encoded via the senses. If you have all of your senses available to you, then you would have visual, olfaction, taste, auditory and touch memories encoded. Very basic sensations are encoded into memory along with other information in the environment. **Encoding Specificity** is the name given to the process whereby specific information is encoded with a particular memory.

For example, every time you hear a particular song you may recall an incident, person, place, object, animal, taste, smell, feeling etc. This will be a result of the specific information that was encoded with that particular song.

At your high school formal you may have had the last dance with a guy or girl that you have always liked, but never acted upon. You may have danced to a certain song, and now, any time you hear that song you instantly remember dancing with your childhood sweetheart, the smell of cologne/perfume, the feeling of closeness, the gentle touch of hands and any other salient information within the environment. These other elements were encoded with the song and so when you hear it now, the song facilitates memory recall of these other stimuli.

Encoded into memory along side 'High School Formal' is all the sights, sounds, smells, emotions, etc of the event. To attempt to recall any particular forgotten memory within that event, you may try to recall other memories surrounding it in the hope of finding one that the lost memory was encoded with. Find a memory that was encoded with it and you stand a great chance of recalling the 'lost' memory.

If you have ever lost your keys and tried to recall where you put them, you may have adopted certain strategies to help remember. For example, you may try to retrace your steps in your mind. The mental retracing of steps brings certain information into your short-term memory and with this information other information that was encoded at the same time. You may have put your keys down next to the telephone on answering a call. When you retrace your steps and remember the phone call, it is likely that you shall recall putting the keys down, as these two chunks of information were encoded together. This is basically how Encoding Specificity works.

**Information is encoded into memory along with other salient stimuli present.**

So, how does the actor utilise this theory of Encoding Specificity? In a number of ways, but first lets have a brief look at processes that help us to learn.

There are three main 'control' processes which facilitate learning. They are **Rehearsal, Coding** and **Imaging**.

**Rehearsal** is a fairly shallow form of encoding information, with the data being processed by rote. If you were to try to remember a phone number by constantly repeating it to yourself, you would be utilising a rehearsal method to facilitate learning. In your childhood you most likely learnt the alphabet by rote; many acting coaches teach that this method of learning lines is wrong and should not be employed for acting purposes. I disagree with this line of thought and will expand on 'why' later on.

**Coding** is the second method for the facilitation of learning. Coding occurs when certain information to be remembered is put in context with information that is easily retrievable. For example you may have remembered the order of the planets in our Solar System, away from the sun, by the following sentence. "My Very Earnest Mother Just Showed Us Nine Planets." Mercury, Venus, Earth, Mars, Jupiter, Saturn, Uranus, Neptune & Pluto.

**Imaging** is the creation of visual images in order to remember verbal, or possibly acoustic, information. For example if you wanted to remember that you had exams on Friday and Sunday you may picture yourself with a *book* while *frying* some eggs out in the *sun*.

For this course we do not use the coding nor Imaging methods as stated above. Instead we utilise off-chutes of these in the form of;

`Encoding Specificity', Reality Visualization and Imagination Visualization to aid a character's recall of past events;

Rehearsal, with particular caution paid to encoding specificity;

And; Behavioural improvisation on the set script with many and varied 'Others'.

## Line Memorization

Cast your mind back only moments ago when we were discussing Encoding Specificity. We saw that information is encoded into memory along side other salient information within the encoding environment. This is **IMPORTANT** to remember.

\*\*\*\*\*\*\*

**The Environment that surrounds you when memorising your script may be instrumental to your performance!**
\*\*\*\*\*\*\*

Have you ever learnt lines at home only to find that when you got to your rehearsal the lines wouldn't come? You probably said to people;

"But I know them; I had them down perfectly at home!"

Yes, you knew them perfectly *at home*! But you're not now at home, you're in a different environment devoid of all the stimuli that were encoded along side those lines. This makes recall very hard.

Most actors that I have dealt with memorise their lines looking at the page, not 'connecting' with anything particular, (emotionally, intellectually or otherwise) and quite often they practice ways of saying the lines, trying out inflections until finally settling on one particular delivery. If this is you then I have great news! You now have the opportunity to try a very different style of script learning that will greatly improve your performance.

Firstly, don't look at your script while delivering lines, don't say them to yourself with your eyes immersed on the page. In this instance what is encoded into your memory is;

'Looking down at script reading lines.'

The chances of this being a similar environment to that of recall, (Performance) is extremely slim. Also, if you are placing any particular inflections onto the dialogue these inflections are also encoded into memory.

Why is this bad? If you memorise lines with certain inflections that will almost certainly be the way in which the lines are finally delivered. Great actors are truthful to the moment; they interact in the moment of performance. If you have encoded your lines in a particular way then your performance will be a result of an **idea** of what you **thought** the scene was about at some point in the past. What you want to discover is what is the scene about **now**!

You may have learnt your lines in the past with a particular inflection and when you came to the rehearsal the director asked you to do it differently. In this situation you may have found it hard to break the encoded vocal pattern, frustrating you and the director. Not good.

You may have been in a performance run for a while and found yourself getting 'stale'. This is another indicator that you are performing from the past and not truly from the 'now'.

Acting, for me, is about staying true to the current interaction. To do this you must have virtually infinite flexibility with your lines and be honestly connected with the 'Other'. The way you deliver a line, the inflections etc, should not be pre-planned but merely a result of yourself living and reacting honestly in the current given circumstances, off the 'Other'. This means that if some-one sneezes you don't ignore it, if the other actor starts a coughing fit which has never happened before, by staying connected to them and having vocal flexibility with the lines you can give this scene unique life.

**What the scene is about is defined during its enactment.**

Yes, you can have ideas about what you think the scene is about, but for the unique performance in the 'now', you'll only be able to comment on what the scene was actually about *after* it has been played out. For the most part there will only be minor variations across performances, but it's these variations, that are a result of being in the moment, that gives the performance its unique life.

You should know your lines as well as you know the alphabet. Only when you know them without having to use any cognitive resources to aid in recall can you then truly live in the situation. The inspirational freedom gained from knowing your lines to this level is absolutely wonderful. Just '*knowing*' your lines is not enough; you should know them like your own name.

Words, lines, dialogue, all have a meaning on the page, they have literary value. However, the performance is not literature, it is living, breathing life and as such the meanings of words are only discovered through their expression, they have no universal intrinsic meaning.

The words, "I love you" in the performance may mean; "I hate you" or "I want to sleep with you" or "Thanks for the coffee" or "You've got to be joking" or numerous other interpretations all depending upon the actual delivery and given circumstance of the scene.

Be careful not to pre-judge the meanings of words when in literature form. Find their meanings in performance for that is where they will be defined in their intended state.

So how do you learn your lines then? How do you encode your lines so as to support living honestly during the performance? How do you give yourself almost infinite creative vocal flexibility for delivery? How do you not pre-judge the meanings of the intended spoken word when read in literature? Read on...

*Robert Carne*
**Rules of Memorization**

**RULE 1:**
  Never repeat your lines while looking at the page.

  One of the last things that you want is to become dependent on your script. Looking at your script will see the page encoded into memory along with the lines. Ideally you would have someone telling you your lines in a neutral tone so that the script isn't even in your hand. You would then wait about five to seven seconds, take a few breaths and run the line. This is great when you can do it unfortunately it isn't always practical. Alternatively, look at the page, take in a sentence or so into short-term memory, then look away from the page, breath and wait at least five seconds and then deliver your lines.

  Once you have delivered your lines, wait a few seconds to take in the 'Other's' reaction, react, and then look back to the page and continue. If learning with someone else, make sure that you are looking at them while they deliver their lines and vice versa. The reason that you wait at least five seconds before delivering lines is to allow time for the lines to transfer from your acoustic memory into your Short Term memory. Once in Short Term memory the lines have a better chance of crossing into your Long Term memory.

**RULE 2:**
  Always honestly connect with an 'Other' while delivering your lines.

  When learning your lines what do we actually want encoded with them? We want to encode lines into memory in a way that will allow us to honestly connect with the 'Other' when we are performing. So, after you have taken the lines into your short term memory, looked away and breathed you then need to honestly connect with an 'Other'. Once you have connected you then deliver your line/s being connected. Encoded into memory will be the line **and** being connected to an 'Other'.

**RULE 3:**

Throughout your line memorisation, each time you deliver your lines, find a new 'Other' and have a different 'Preparation' (We will look at Preparation in depth in the next Chapter) for that unique interaction.

The previous rule told you to connect with an 'Other' while reciting the line, what you also need to do is deliver the line differently every time you rehearse it by connecting with a different, 'Other'.

This is important because if you kept the same 'Other' each time you rehearsed, the line would be encoded with a particular 'Other' rather than a unique one, fresh in the 'now'. If you rehearse with another actor just make certain that your preparations are different each time, and in effect you will have a different 'Other'.

You have to see and connect honestly each time. What is now encoded into memory is the line along side staying connected to this 'Other' in this unique situation. By the time you have learnt your lines you will have performed them with dozens of different 'Others', the encoding will not be specific to any particular one and so will be fresh each time. When you are on stage/screen you will be doing exactly what you have been doing all along throughout the learning process, staying connected to the 'Other' in a unique situation, within the given circumstance of another story, reacting in the 'now' to anything that may occur.

**RULE 4:**

Be creative with your given circumstances, intellectual preparations and emotional preparations. Take the lines outside of the scripted environment.

Be creative! Drop the circumstances of the script and get inside the words in a variety of situations. Rehearse your lines; With the cat; In the shower; Doing the ironing; While playing Monopoly; On the bus; Doing push-ups; Making a cake; On the toilet; Combing your hair; Driving the car; Walking the dog; Cleaning your ears; Swimming laps; In bed; While fixing the car; Playing with your belly button; While having a drink; At a funeral; Squeezing a zit; Playing table tennis; With a stuffed toy; Standing on your head; Playing Cards; Etc...

Basically you are improvising behavior around set dialogue.

**Allow the unique environment, situation and behaviour to effect the line's delivery.**

Each time you rehearse find a new intellectual and emotional preparation. We will look at these preparations in the next Chapter.

**RULE 5:**
Find the delivery though the behaviour.

This continues the theme of the last rule. Allow the different behaviours stemming from the situations to effect how the lines are delivered. The lines should come out differently if you are determined to win an arm wrestle to when you are trying to seduce the cat! Don't worry too much about the 'meanings' of the words. The meaning will come from the situation and behaviour. Have fun discovering new meanings to the script. You are rehearsing your lines, this is not your end performance. If you rehearse your end performance you will find it near impossible to truly stay connected in the 'now' when you finally get there. You will, I re-iterate, merely perform from an idea of what you thought the scene was about sometime in the past.

**RULE 6:**

Breathe naturally and take your time throughout the delivery of your lines.

Don't try and say your lines quickly or all in one breath. Take your time, relax, breath naturally. By breathing naturally through the behaviour that you are committed to will mean that you breathe naturally during the performance. Let the situation find its own rhythm. This doesn't necessarily mean that the lines will always be delivered slowly; it just means that they are not necessarily quick. All in good time through the behaviour.

**RULE 7:**

If memorising for film or TV, where possible rehearse with a camera present.

Another thing I'm often confronted with by actors is the complaint that they know their lines at home and rehearsing with friends, but when they get in front of a camera they dry up. This again goes back to the fundamentals of Encoding Specificity.

I was on the set of a commercial one day when a model, who wanted to get more into the acting side of the industry, broached this dilemma to me. I simply said;

"If you find trouble remembering your lines when you get in front of a camera then start rehearsing and memorising your lines **in front of a camera!**"

The look on her face was wonderful, she looked a little bit embarrassed, such a simple answer but very effective.

So, where possible while you are rehearsing, have a video camera pointed at you. It can just be mounted on a tripod without anyone operating it, it doesn't even have to be turned on! Just get used to it being there. By having it present you will be much more relaxed around the camera when performing for the actual shoot.

**RULE 8:**

Probably the most important rule of all, **HAVE FUN**!!!

Have fun giving yourself different situations, make them as creative or bizarre as you like. This is not a 'feel-good' rule, this is important! Generally, the more fun you are having the more spontaneous you will be.

This doesn't necessarily mean 'silly' fun, you can play the part of a serial killer and have lots of fun as an actor bringing them to life. In fact you should have fun with every character you play. Remember it's just a character, so HAVE FUN!!!

## Speed Runs

Once you know your lines doing 'Speed Runs' is a great way of firmly embedding them into memory. A Speed Run is basically where you recite your lines as fast as you can.

I mentioned earlier that many acting coaches look down upon learning via the rehearsal method, or rote. Speed Runs are a form of rote rehearsal and my reasons for disagreeing with them should be made apparent by the following.

## *Rules of Speed Runs*

**RULE 1:**

Recite your lines as fast as you can; only stopping to breathe when you need to.

As you perform a number of Speed Runs, make sure that you are not breathing in the same places each time. If you do breath at the same time then this will become a sticking point during performance, you'll get into the 'habit' of breathing at that point. So, random breath points over your various speed runs.

**RULE 2:**

Line delivery should be void of any 'meaning'.

When delivering the lines all you are doing is getting words out, one after the other. It should sound like a stream, a barrage of words without purpose, without texture, without substance.

**RULE 3:**

Totally ignore punctuation during Speed Runs.

Make certain that you are not pausing at full stops or commas. Ensure that no inflections enter into your vocal range. If you find that you are stopping at a full stop or pausing at a comma, go over the dialogue again, consciously making certain that the speed and constancy during a sentence, is the same as across sentences. Remember, these are all just words without meaning, no inflections, inflections will add meaning and meaning will be encoded into memory thus putting barriers between you and truly living in the moment during performance.

The idea of Speed Runs is to bed the lines firmly into memory, to make them come out as easily as the alphabet, without any conscious thought.

**Once you know your lines without conscious thought, then you can really start to act!**

Think of dialogue like the canvas for a painter. The lines of dialogue are the canvas upon which you will paint your performance.

The painter has to stretch their canvas firmly onto a sturdy frame; they must secure it making certain that it is tight, even and uniform across the total surface. The artist wouldn't dream of starting to paint until this basic foundation was perfect. So are the lines with the actor. Go into every performance with a well-made canvas. If you know your lines without conscious thought then you can step upon the stage or set and be free to interact honestly from moment to moment living truly with your 'Others'. If you don't know them that well then your freedom will be restricted and your potential not reached.

Don't be lazy! I can't stress enough how important it is to know your lines without conscious effort. You should know them to this level at least by two weeks before Opening night for a stage play and as soon as possible for television and film. (Sometimes your script can get to you very late indeed!) You don't know how much fun acting can really be until you've performed with lines memorised perfectly and without any encoded restrictions on meaning. The freedom is truly one of the most amazing experiences you'll ever have.

### *Behaviour*

We recently touched briefly on Behaviour while learning your lines; let's now go in to a bit more detail.

Most, if not all, creatures are in a constant state of behaviour. As humans we are thinking about things, we are talking, we are sensing different stimuli, we are engaged in physical activities from the subtle scratch to the triple back flip! From and through these Behaviours we communicate. We flirt, we dominate, we scare, and we are scared. Now as actors we want to ensure that our characters are engaged in behaviour, it is through these behaviours that our characters will communicate with other characters and the audience.

Dialogue is much more easily delivered and 'truthful' if it is spoken through the 'doing', through the behaviour of the character connected to an 'Other'. Many, many successful actors know and use this knowledge to great effect; some have even got into a habit across different characters of using the same behaviour. I have met many actors that use the behaviour of smoking to help them in their natural delivery of dialogue. I urge you not to restrict yourselves to a few behavioural 'tricks' but instead encourage you to discover new and unique behaviours for your character traits all the while allowing your 'connected' performance to elicit fresh behaviour in the moment.

Let's now create a fictitious character and give them behavioural traits through our understanding of the Interaction, Personal Space, Status and vulnerabilities.

Tom is a shy man; he had very little social interaction as a child and as such has grown up being Socially Vulnerable. Tom also happens to be an intellectual genius. His comprehension of physics and astronomy is renowned around the world and he has written numerous papers that have changed our views on the universe.

So, we now have Tom as Socially and Emotionally Vulnerable. As Socially Vulnerable we may choose to have him interacting with his Personal Space in a general state of Shallow. His physicality would focus slightly inward as he peers out through a barrier that is close to him. Since his Personal Space is Shallow, and thus quite protective, we see him as Interactionally, Low Status. Maybe some people who have read and studied his work and then met him for the first time have been a bit shocked. This person, whom they viewed and thought about in a very socially high status light, is now seen physically portrayed as low status.

As Emotionally Vulnerable Tom's main barrier is of an intellectual nature. What physical trait might we give him? Looking at the Interaction Model you will see that the highest point of intellectual activity is in the Evaluation Stage and is characterised by a shifting of weight or an off-centeredness. Let's make this aspect fairly subtle and just have his head slightly tilted to the side while conversing. (Some classic characters with similar vulnerabilities to Tom, who have had much less subtle traits are, Raymond, from the film, `Rainman' played by Dustin Hoffman; John Nash from the film, 'A Beautiful Mind' played by Russell Crowe).

Vocally let's pitch his voice a bit higher than 'normal', (unsure stage), and have dialogue delivered slightly hesitantly to further enhance his evaluatory nature.

By living in this behavioural circumstance for a while, the physicality will in turn effect the way you feel and you will become comfortable interacting in this way. Once you are comfortable and 'in' their body, you can then find the freedom of exploring the behavioural nuances that come 'in-the-moment'.

Allow yourself to discover what it is to be that person/character interacting in life. Maybe during one rehearsal another actor is wearing a shirt that has a particular colour pattern that closely resembles an interstellar nebular. Perhaps you allow your head to tilt more as you go in closer to inspect it, all the while delivering the dialogue through this new and unique interaction. Maybe you take a big risk and take his or her shirt off them and lay it on a table to more closely examine it. Have fun, discover in the moment.

Props and physical items, like the shirt, can be the source of wonderful behaviours that help you to more honestly live in the moment. Like the behaviour of smoking, find things that help you to relax and live in the character. Maybe your character eats Tic Tacs a lot; maybe they play with their hair; or roll dice; or pull their hands inside their jumpers; or pick fluff off their coats; or scratch their bum; or are very expressive with their hands; or rub their hands a lot because of poor circulation; or ....?

Now we may have decided to base Tom's physicality in a higher status area such as in the Realization/Acceptance Stage of the Interaction. He may still be in `Shallow' for his Personal Space, however, his body weight will be Centred and his voice lower without hesitation. Or you may decide to concoct a weird and wonderful mix of vocal, physicality and Personal Space, full of contradictions, just to see what happens, to experiment, to learn, to have fun!

## *Vocal Behavior*

Another behaviour, which is often overlooked, is non-dialogue verbal behaviour. In our everyday interactions we are constantly making vocal noises and sounds that are not a part of our spoken text. These include sounds like;

Ummm, Ahhh, Ohhhh, Haaa, Hmmm, Uha, and many more sounds which are too hard to try and spell!

Even though I firmly believe in 'sticking to the script', while keeping connected to the 'Other', don't overlook the sounds that will help bring the scene to life. For some reason when many students, and even professionals, get a script in their hands they keep their vocality to the words written and don't allow any other sounds to come out. We all know what it's like to be agreeing within someone by nodding our head and saying Mmmmm while they are speaking. When acting, allow yourself the freedom to explore these gutturals, allow sounds to come out, if you are honestly connected to your 'Other' then this should be fairly easy. Also allow for the behaviour that accompanies them, like nodding the head. Acting doesn't cease when you stop talking!

Another common sound is made when someone is telling you a story about a situation in their life; they communicate certain dialogue and there is a catalyst, suddenly everything they have been talking about makes sense. As they continue speaking you make the sound – Ahhhhhhhh while nodding your head. You should always allow these overlapping of sounds with another's dialogue to come freely in Theatre. Sometimes you can't do it in Television or Film because of the nightmares it can create in editing, but if they are using multiple cameras, or are sticking to a single shot, then do it! If you are unsure about how any sounds will cut in editing, check with the director. Honest, connected, non-dialogue vocal reactions can really bring a scene to life. It's a part of living in the moment.

One final word on gutturals, you must be sure that your sounds do not obscure the other persons dialogue unless it is intended to do so. Gutturals are the icing, **not** the cake.

## Visualization for Character Recall

Another aspect in acting concerning memory is seen when a character is recalling past events. We are going to look at two main ways of helping this memory recall; **Reality Visualization** and **Imaginative Visualization**. We will also look at the combining of these two techniques.

### Reality Visualization

First I'd like you to take a moment and without leaving your spot, work out how many windows are in your house or unit. Then read on.

You may have noticed that as you counted the windows you were mentally going through the building, counting as you went. You conjured up a visual representation of your dwelling in your mind and simply counted them.

When enacting a scene where your character is recalling events, it helps to have a memory in place to recount from. This memory can either be created from a real memory or an imagined one.

Let's say that you are playing the part of our hero 'Herman' in an upcoming play. In one particular scene, while conversing with Bradley, you have to recall the events surrounding, and including, your first kiss with Rhonda. The 'Given Circumstances' (that information given by the script) is found in Herman's duologue with Bradley, which follows;

### HERMAN

There we were, sitting near the fountain... just sitting... not even talking. And I feel this thing on my leg. So I go to brush it off... but she's got her hand on my leg! I look at her. She looks at me. She smiles... My heart is thumping. I take her hand...

### BRADLEY

Yes...

### HERMAN

I lean forward...

### BRADLEY

And...

### HERMAN

And... she is the most amazing kisser!

### BRADLEY

Then what?!

### HERMAN

I don't remember, her brother Tony knocked me out with a lump of wood...

So this is what the script has told us, the 'Given Circumstances'.

For the preparation of this scene you may decide to use **Reality Visualization**. Reality Visualization would see you and the actor playing Rhonda and possibly, but not necessarily, the actor playing Tony, going on location near a fountain and acting out the scene for real. (Note if the actor playing Tony is a 'Method actor' be careful he doesn't actually clobber you!)

Once you've acted out this scene in a real location, when retelling the events to Bradley on stage you can draw from actual memories, this obviously makes it easier for you and hopefully more 'truthful' for the audience. As you recall the events you take them straight from your own experience, conjuring up the images in your mind as you retell the story.

### Imaginative Visualization

Alternatively you may decide to use **Imaginative Visualization**. Imaginative Visualization would see you taking time in the rehearsal period to vividly go through the events in your own mind, creating the images as you go. Once on stage in character, you would recall these images that you had previously conjured up in your imagination and retell the story to Bradley using this 'Other'.

Finally you may choose to use a combination of the two. I generally find this to be the most useful, practical and effective method. Let's say that after Herman was knocked out he woke up in a spaceship surrounded by small grey alien beings who subjected him to all manner of 'probes'.

Now, it's a bit impractical to create a full alien spaceship set, hire costumes, props and other actors just to give you some images to work from when telling your tale. In this instance you may well use Reality Visualization for the recollection of events with Rhonda and Imaginative Visualization for our alien friends.

Whichever way you decide to work it is very helpful that you actually do recall into your mind images, or stimuli, from which to draw your performance. Don't merely pretend to remember something, not only is it ineffective but it's also a lot more work than just bringing the images back into consciousness. By actually bringing the images into your mind, you are honestly connecting with an 'Other'.

While usually of a visual nature these concepts also work for the other senses. Your character may be recalling a sound that they heard the night before, or a smell, sensation or taste. Treat these in the same way that you would the visual.

**Note;** to further enrich an artificial memory in performance, add other senses to the memory. For example when Herman is recounting his experience with Rhonda, you may bring other senses to bear on the performance. We have already mentioned the beating heart – a physical sensation. On another level you may decide to pause after;

"I take her hand"

And breathe in through your nose as if remembering the smell of her perfume. Maybe you relax slightly as the sound of the bubbling fountain comes back to you.

By now you've probably realized how beneficial the Reality Visualization can be. You may discover numerous wonderful sensations by **actually being there**. You may not **think** of perfume but if the actress is wearing some when you do this exercise, assuming that you are staying connected with your 'Other', then you will experience this sensation. Taking this one step further you may decide to ask the actress if she would mind wearing that perfume during the actual performances to further strengthen the reality.

Have fun discovering different sensations and stimuli that will enhance your performance. Put yourself in the situations and let in those 'Others!'

*Robert Carne*

**A short sidetrack;** You've probably come into contact at various times in your life with Shakespeare's work. I've only performed in a couple of his plays, Hamlet and A Mid Summer Night's Dream, but have read and seen others as well as performed a number of his soliloquies. I've also spoken to many actors, directors and dramaturges about Shakespeare's plays and particularly about how they may have initially been performed. When engaging in this kind of theorising you really need to think about the circumstances in which the plays were staged and what were the actor's 'Others'.

Let's assume that the play 'Hamlet' was first staged in a theatre similar to this;

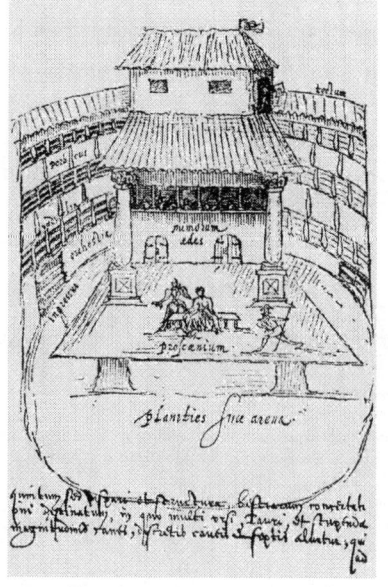

This is a drawing of the Swan Theatre stage area, c.1596, by Johannes de Witt, copied by Arend van Buchell. This is very like the Globe Theatre in which Shakespeare performed many of his plays. You'll notice that there is no roof over the auditorium; this means that the audience would have been lit equally as the performers. (Although it is possible that the building was aligned such that when the performances were staged in the afternoon, most of the seating was in shadow while the stage was lit. Just a thought)

In any case the audience would be much more illuminated than in a modern Theatre where you are, for the most part, in darkness with the actors being lit from powerful stage lighting rigs.

So, immediately there may be a focus problem. The layout of the Theatre may dictate a certain style of performance. What do we have today that may be similar to this environment? The first thing that springs to my mind is a shopping Center performance where everyone is equally lit. Generally the style of acting in these venues is quite amplified as the performers draw people's attention to the stage.

Okay, so let's say for arguments sake that the actors could clearly see the audience. The patrons at the foot of the stage, the 'Groundlings', were from the lower socio-economic suburbs, as this was the area for the cheapest tickets; keep this in mind for the following.

Now, going back to Imaginative Visualization. One day while I was rehearsing a soliloquy from Hamlet, I started imagining myself on stage in the old Globe Theatre. Here are a few lines from the soliloquy that is delivered to the audience.

> "Now might I do it, pat, now he is praying;
> And now I'll do't; and so he goes to heaven:
> And am I then reveng'd? ..."

(Hamlet Act 3, Scene 3)

Note; this punctuation was put in by scholars **after** the fact and was not Shakespeare's.

Without going into the whole story, what has basically been happening up to this moment is that Hamlet has found himself with good reason to kill his Stepfather but has been putting it off. In this scene Hamlet sees an opportunity to kill him while his Stepfather is prone, on his knees praying.

So there I am, at home, imagining myself entering onto stage in front of a group of equally lit rowdy groundlings. I connect with them. They see my situation. I hear them shout at me;

"Kill him ya mug! Get it over with and stop pouncing' about!"

I react in a shaky voice;
"**Now?**"

Again I hear those voices;
"Yes, now ya big girl"

Again I react to them;
"**Might I do it pat? Now he is praying?**"
('pat' basically meaning now)

That crowd keeps it up.
"Ohhhh, yes now! Just do it!"

I hesitantly make my way towards my stepfather,
"**And now I'll do't**"

There are cheers from the crowd. I continue towards my stepfather, dagger raised, all the while trying desperately to come up with an excuse to put it off. Suddenly an idea strikes me, I stop and turn back to the groundlings;

"**And so he goes to heaven,**"

A groan from the audience.

"**And am I then revenged?**"

And I then go on and try to justify my position to the audience.

Now you may be horrified at this interpretation. Or maybe suddenly it makes sense. Me, I had fun and it made sense at the time and it would have been a truthful theatrical performance, whether or not it has ever been performed as such is besides the point, the important thing is in the discovery and learning.

Cast off your pre-conceptions, keep an open mind and anything is possible. By putting myself into an imaginary situation suddenly I was gaining insights to possible interpretations of the script. I mentioned earlier that the punctuation was not Shakespeare's but a scholar's. This is important, don't let the punctuation on the page; the literary identity of the script, dictate the performance identity. It may aid you in your understanding, but don't allow it to rule your performance.

## Recounting the Memory

Back to memory and a general rule about recounting memories in performance.

Quite often in life when retelling a particularly hurtful memory we draw our personal space inward, giving us protection while divulging information that has effected our vulnerabilities. We may avoid eye contact, head lowered, possibly trying to hide the tears that are doing their best to force their way through as we do **our best** to bury the emotion. Now while this is generally the case in life, in performance we usually want to share our character's plight with the audience and let them into our pain, our struggle. How do we do that?

Instead of withdrawing your character's Personal Space into Shallow, or closer, allow the Personal Space to push outwards over the audience. (Film, TV or Theatre) When you do this, your character becomes vulnerable to the audience and inside your personal space thus letting them into your trials rather than shutting them out. So as a general rule, don't look down or withdraw your Personal Space when finding the memories, find the memories while looking out, with your Personal Space extended.

## Script Analysis

I don't go into great depth on script analysis, the reason being I'm very much a believer of finding the meaning through the enacting of the scene, rather than studying the literary piece and Intellectualizing possibilities. Having said that, we will look at a number of useful approaches when confronting a script, some for meaning analysis, but mainly for character detail.

### Confronting a Script

You have just received your script, what now? The first thing to do is find yourself a nice relaxed environment, where you won't be distracted, to read the script in it's entirety. You might go to the park or your backyard, anywhere where you can relax. Take a pen and some paper with you; you'll need it when you've finished reading. Next, turn off your mobile phone and take any normal phones off the hook. The world can live without you for a couple of hours.

Once you have settled yourself into this environment, read the script all the way through for enjoyment. Have fun, you only ever get one first read of a script, make the most out of it as first impressions are important.

After you have finished reading the script, make notes on any thoughts or feelings you have had regarding the story as a whole.

Write down how you felt about the plot and how things transpired though the story. Is it Story or Character driven? Did you cry? Laugh? Feel inspired? Did it make you want to go out and do something? Did it make you angry? What we want to find in this reading is your reaction to the piece without any huge intellectualization. How did the story effect you?

Write about your character and how they made you feel or think. Write about other characters that you interact with. Write about anything that sticks in your mind about the story or characters. You will only ever get one first read of a script and it is an important one, just like the audience will only have one first experience with the production.

Next you need to glean specific character information from the script. This information will serve as the basis for further character creation. So read the script again, (It doesn't have to be the same day) making extensive notes along the way and highlighting such things as;

What does the writers notes say about your character?

**As the character;**

What do you say about yourself? What do other characters say about you? What do you say about other characters? What are your relationships with the other characters? What are all your personal details – age, likes, dislikes, basically anything else concerning your character.

You now have all of your characters' 'Given Circumstances'; you have all that the writer has given you.

## *Intellectualizing Meaning in the Script*

Many people break up the scenes into 'Beats' or 'Bits'. (Taken from the Stanislavski Method) I sometimes do this but generally don't. Beats are very commonly used in conventional acting. Beats are basically units of meaning. So every-time there is a thought change, there is a new beat. Actors who use this will then make a little mark (/) in their script. This, theoretically, helps the actor to focus on the changes and glean meaning from the script. Try this approach, if it works for you then use it. If I am having trouble with a scene I will sometimes try breaking it into beats just to get a fresh angle on it. Here's a quick example of a short scene broken into Beats. (Bits)

"Now/ might I do it, pat, now he is praying;/
And now I'll do't;/ and so he goes to heaven:/
And am I then reveng'd?/ Why that would be scann'd: A villain kills my father; and, for that, I, his sole son, do this same villain send to heaven./ Why, this is hire and salary, not revenge.(Hamlet Act 3, Scene 3)

Note, actors find the Beats in different places, some have a beat after every punctuation, if I use this method I take the beat at my perceived change of thought.

The reason that I generally don't use beats is that I want to discover the changes while I am actually engaged in the lines, not from just thinking about them. So while I am learning my lines I am playing with numerous interpretations, (while connected to the 'other' etc...) and I thus discover meaning through that process. I find that the discoveries made are much richer than those just thought up totally outside of the behaviour.

### *Set-up and Target Dialogue*

In life we often use Set-up dialogue to give background information to the Target dialogue; the important information.

For example; "I was walking in the park the other day and I saw Herman kissing Rhonda!"

In this piece the Set-up dialogue is:

"I was walking in the park the other day ..."

This information, for this example, is trivial, the important aspect is:

"... Herman kissing Rhonda!"

If these were lines of dialogue in a script, you would place very little emphasis on, "I was walking in the park the other day ..." these words would probably be delivered quite quickly as you want to get to the Target dialogue as soon as possible, the juicy part! Emphasis, or importance, would then be placed upon the Target dialogue, "... I saw Herman kissing Rhonda!"

When looking at a scene you may like to try isolating the Set-up dialogue and the Target dialogue. I use this technique more often than 'Beats' as not only do we discover meaning but also importance. Here is a bit more, the Target dialogue is in Bold.

"I was walking in the park the other day and I saw **Herman kissing Rhonda**! Can you believe it? They were **kissing**! Now I'm not much of a gossip but I had to tell you because... **Tony just found out**! Thought you'd like to know."

Try delivering those lines out loud, say the Set-up dialogue quickly, and slow down and emphasise the Target dialogue.

That's it for script analysis. I know, not much, but it's all you'll really need. These techniques are just for when you get stuck on a particular scene, they can be very helpful but you're better off finding this information in the enacting of the scene, in the behaviour. Don't over Intellectualize the script; put nearly all of your resources into the character creation and general preparation. The scene should be alive in the 'Now', take the risk and find it in-the-moment!

*Robert Carne*
## Rehearsal and Performance Thresholds

As is the case with learning your lines, I see rehearsals as a place to explore your character through different behaviours in-the-moment. Play around with interpretations but never lock in a 'way' of doing it. As you explore your character through the rehearsal process both with the other actors and in your own time, you will make discoveries that are in line with the Director's objective for the piece and your Character. These Character behavioural discoveries that 'work' should not become 'locked in' as part of your performance but should be seen as *'potentials'* that may come to fruition given what happens in-the-moment during performances. As you rehearse your Character many potentials will arise. These potentials will now have a low threshold during the performance and should you find yourself in a situation that is conducive to the realization of a potential then giving it life will come naturally as a result of being in-the-moment. The rehearsal process allows you to explore these potentials giving you a pool of character resources upon which to draw should the moment present.

### Practical Exercises

I want you to start being aware of the cues that trigger memories for you. I'm sure you've had the situation while talking to someone where you are both unsure of exactly how you got onto a particular topic.

Watch people as they are recalling a situation from their life, see where their eyes travel. Generally speaking they will look away while searching for the memory and then to you when delivering it. The looking away facilitates the evaluation, and the looking at you sees them connect with their other for your response.

Go and find a monologue, with a visual recall aspect to it, and learn it. Learn it properly and learn it almost as well as you know the alphabet. Don't worry about the meaning in performance, have fun and learn it without tying it to any specific 'Other'.

Once you know the monologue dialogue well enough that you can speed run it without the slightest hesitation then try some Visualization techniques for the appropriate section of the piece.

When you have some firm established Visualizations, look into the script for any Set-up or Target dialogue. Highlight in green any Set-up dialogue and in red any target dialogue. Go over the piece again a number of times, and again connected to varying 'Others' but this time take into account your Set-up and Target dialogue.

Perform your monologue to an audience. Any audience; family, friends, other actors, whoever. It doesn't matter if your performance is bad, average or Academy Award material, the main thing for now is that you are performing.

# CHAPTER 7

## *Preparation and Recovery*

It's alright now ... I'm fine... Honest

*Robert Carne*
**Preparation**

While Preparation consists of all work done on a character prior to performance, this Chapter will be primarily concerned with those 'preparations' needed immediately before performing. Indeed, in reality, this whole course is on Preparation for performance.

In the first Chapter we identified four main attributes of 'self': Spiritual, Physical, Emotional and Intellectual. These are the four areas we need to address in preparation for performance.

**Spiritual Preparation**

I've started with Spiritual because it is an area very specific and personal to the individual. I don't know your personal religion, beliefs or ideologies and as you are aware these can be very emotive topics. It is primarily for these reasons that I am only going to touch lightly in this area and leave it for you to explore further.

If it is your knowledge, or belief, that a God plays a part in your life, then get them on side during the rehearsal process and particularly just prior to performance. Say a prayer, ask for strength, do whatever you need to do to have your God beside you as you act.

If you have no knowledge, or belief that a God plays a part in your life, then find the essence of who you are and allow your own personal energy to be fully focused on your performance.

If your character has a similar spirituality to yourself then great, makes things much easier. Even if your character's beliefs are quite different it may still pose no problem if you have no hesitation in taking on those beliefs in a role. However, if you have strong spiritual beliefs in one area and your character has strong in another, and there is intrinsic conflict, then there **may** be a problem.

For example: There are many people who would find it spiritually blasphemous to play a possessed, Satanistic Devil worshiper. My advice is if you have spiritual conflicts with a character that concerns you and will effect your enacting thereof, don't play the role. It's as simple as that. Don't sacrifice your own morality, spirituality or beliefs for the sake of a performance, there'll be plenty more roles.

As you can see, the spiritual aspect to your acting really needs to be formulated by you. Think about it, think about the sort of characters that you would not like to play for spiritual reasons and think about how you can use your own spirituality to help bring a character to life.

The spirituality of a character may play a big part in their life. How do their beliefs differ from yours? How are they similar? Find parallels between your spirituality and the character's, this will give you ways into their spiritual life via your own beliefs.

Most of the time your character's spirituality will not even be mentioned and won't have any effect on your portrayal of that character at all, so don't concern yourself too much with this side. I needed to include this section just to make you aware that it can be an issue at times.

## Physical Preparation

The main thing with a physical preparation is to be sure that your body is flexible enough to allow for the full effortless movement range of your character.

## Stretching

Stretch. Do some basic stretches to limber up before a performance. Here are some good easy stretches that will cover most characters. Obviously if your character is an Olympic Gymnast, or a dancer or some other very agile person then your physical preparation may need more attention.

Before stretching, warm up your muscles with some running on the spot, (approximately 3 minutes) and star-jumps (approximately 100). Be very careful while stretching, don't overexert, when you feel the stretch working, hold that position for a count of fifteen, relax, give it a gentle shake and then stretch again.

If you are new to stretching don't get over enthusiastic with your efforts. Relax and be patient, flexibility takes time. The last thing you want to do is pull a hamstring or strain a muscle on opening night! Take it easy, closely monitor yourself. Your body will tell you when enough is enough. By the same token make sure that you can feel the stretch, don't go the other way and be lazy, a nice firm stretch that you can feel working the muscles and tendons.

**NOTE:** All exercises are done at your own risk, so be careful! If in any doubt, don't do the exercise.

**Groin Stretch**

Start with a gentle groin stretch. Sitting on the ground, feet together, and knees out. Keeping your back straight gently push your knees downward while lifting up and over with the torso. Hold this stretch for fifteen seconds and then relax for a moment. Repeat.

**Neck Stretch**

Next, cross your legs, place your hands on the ground behind you and gently tilt your head to one side. Hold this stretch for fifteen seconds and then change sides. Repeat.

## Back Stretch

While sitting cross your legs and then place your left foot behind your right knee, insert your right arm through the hole under your left knee, place your left hand on the ground behind you and gently twist the torso to the left. Hold this position for a count of fifteen and then change sides. Repeat.

## Arm Stretch

Place your right arm horizontally across your body, take your left forearm and gently pull your right arm towards your body. Hold this position for a count of fifteen and then change sides. Repeat.

## Hamstring Stretch

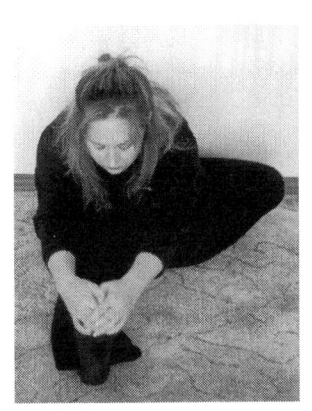

Stretch your right leg out in front of you with your left foot touching your right knee. Keeping the back of your right knee on the ground, gently stretch your torso over the top of your right leg, moving your chin towards your toes.

Don't worry if you can't reach your foot, just grab where you can. Hold this position for a count of fifteen and then change sides. Repeat.

### Calf Stretch

Standing up, move your right foot out in front of your body and bend your right knee. Place both hands on top of your right leg. While keeping your left heal on the ground and your left leg straight, gently bend your right knee until you feel a nice stretch in the left calf muscle. Hold this position for a count of fifteen and then change sides. Repeat.

### Quadriceps Stretch

Standing on your left leg, bend your right knee and grab hold of your right foot with your left hand. Keeping your right hand out to the side for balance, gently pull your right foot upwards stretching your Quadriceps muscle. Hold this position for a count of fifteen and then change sides. Repeat.

## Side Stretch

With your legs straight and comfortably apart, raise your right arm up over your head and place your left hand onto your left knee. Stretch the right arm upward and over the body, tilting the torso as you stretch and maintaining the same plane (Like being between two plates of glass). Hold this position for a count of fifteen and then change sides. Repeat.

These stretches should only take five to ten minutes to complete so try to do these exercises daily to help keep you loose and ready for the physical demands of any role. You may be a dancer or gymnast or maybe you do yoga, if so utilize the stretches that you enjoy and work well for you. The stretches illustrated are guidelines for you and for those who are new to stretching.

## *Vocal Warm-Up*

Part of your physical preparation is a vocal warm-up. I've put together a few simple vocal warm-ups to work your mouth, vocal cords and diaphragm in preparation for a performance. When doing these exercises ensure that you are connecting in some way to an 'Other', this is to make sure that your body learns to use the benefits of these exercises in 'real' situations, when the mind and focus is on other things.

**Exercise 1:**

This is an important exercise that I want you to master as soon as you can.

Lie on your back, legs not crossed, hands on your diaphragm (lower tummy). Breath so that your hands rise and fall with the breath. Your stomach should rise when you breath in and fall when you breath out.

A lot of you will find this exercise hard. When standing up you should be breathing this way as well, most of you will find that your stomach stays in and your shoulders rise. Take a deep breath and find out where your breath goes. If your chest and shoulders rise then you need to start focusing on getting the breath down into the stomach area (diaphragm).

Why? Well there are a number of reasons. First your breath capacity will increase by freeing up more space for the air. Second, by strengthening the diaphragm you will be better equipped to project your voice. Thirdly, your voice will be placed better so that there is no tension in the neck. The only tense muscle should be your diaphragm. Finally, and for me most importantly, your lower tummy is the area where a lot of unresolved emotions lie. Hmmmm, sounds a bit 'out there' I know, but trust me on this and you'll soon discover for yourself the truth in it.

In times of great emotional turmoil you have probably felt the emotion coming up from deep down in your stomach. You can feel it rise. The next time that you start to feel an emotion coming up, take notice of it. We've all had that near choking feeling in the throat as we've struggled to hold back tears. The emotion is coming up and we try to stop it before it reaches its goal, before we let it out.

You need to breathe down deep to allow your Initial Emotions to effect you. If you have been breathing through movies as I asked in a previous Chapter and have found that it doesn't work for you then it may be because you are not breathing down deep enough. For most of you there will be a lot of stored up emotional 'junk' down there so don't be surprised if emotions start popping up after you've been doing this exercise for a while. You'll probably discover emotions that you'd forgotten you have!

Enjoy all emotions, every one of them. They are a part of being human. Allow yourself, give permission to yourself, to feel. You need to have a full emotional range to reach your potential as an actor.

Once you are breathing in this way, try some of the vocal warm-ups in this position, it is great for a relaxed warm-up before a show.

**Exercise 2:**

I don't remember where I learnt this little vocal pattern from but my thanks goes to the teacher involved. This exercise moves the placement of your voice forwards and backwards in the mouth. Start in the middle, follow the arrows to the right and end back in the middle after a full circuit. Learn this simple diagram off by heart, it's easy but effective.

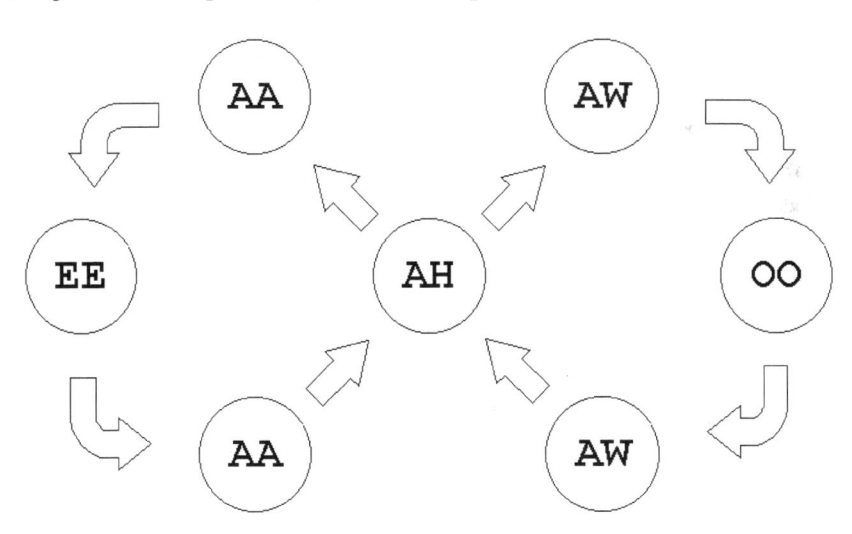

```
         AA              AW

   EE           AH             OO

         AA              AW
```

Once you know this sound pattern, start to put a consonant on the beginning; and when you are comfortable with that put one on the end too. For example:

**zAHp→zAWp→zOOp→zAWp→zAHp→zAAp→zEEp→zAAp→zAHp**

**tAHs→tAWs→tOOs→tAWs→tAHs→tAAs→tEEs→tAAs→tAHs**

When doing this exercise be sure to use the following consonants at the beginning at least once and in this order.

**P    T    C**
**B    D    G**

I use this exercise mostly on my way to a rehearsal, performance or audition. It's a great one for in the car, I look at the number-plates of other vehicles and use the consonants in the vocal loop. This gives me a random factor so that I don't use the same combinations all the time.

This exercise is also very good when used with scales. Go up and down an octave on one sound and then move on to the next. This not only works the mouth but also your range.

**Exercise 3**

This one I learnt from Shelley Bissett in the car one day. This is a simple exercise to place your voice at the front of your mouth. Take a deep breath and as you exhale at a constant rate make a Sssssssssssss sound. Keep going until you are out of breath and then repeat it a few times.

**Exercise 4**

Here's one to get your top lip moving. Pinch the full width of your top lip with your thumb and forefinger. Then, recite dialogue for two to three minutes. Take your fingers away and you'll feel your top lip starting to work harder.

**Exercise 5**

Another exercise to get your lips moving but also to get your voice placed correctly in the mouth. Open your mouth and with the heels of the palms of your hands, push your cheeks in so that your jaw is forced open. Start reciting dialogue. It should feel like the sound is being made at the front of your mouth. This is a great one for projection. Recite for two to three minutes and then take your hands away. Keep reciting and try to keep the voice placed in the same spot. I love this one! Really works well.

Humming is also good for warming up your vocal apparatus and again humming scales works well.

One of the best places to warm up your voice is in a hot shower. The steam is great for those vocal cords so each morning start the day by warming up your voice in the shower!

**Tongue Twisters**

For tongue, mouth and lips dexterity practice tongue twisters for exercise. Go out and buy the Dr Seuss Book, 'Fox in Sox', read it out loud as often as you can, it is great for verbal dexterity. For now, here are a few tongue twisters to try. Repeat them over and over again quickly.

* **Red Leather, Yellow Leather.**
* **The Leath Police Dismisseth us.**
* **The Big Black Bug, Bled Black Blood.**
* **Six sick Shieks, sixth sick sheep.**
* **Red Lorry, Yellow Lorry.**
* **Betty Boop bounced a bright, blue, basket ball.**
* **Tickey took Tockey to tickle Tackey's toes.**
* **A quick quiet cup of proper coffee, in a quick quiet proper cup of coffee cup.**
* **Tiana's terrific tongue twisters, twisted Tanya's tongue tantalisingly**
* **Caroline's quick quip, quelled Colin's quarrel with Kylie's queer acquaintance.**

*Robert Carne*
## Emotional Preparation

In this section you're going to look at the emotional states that you need to address before a particularly emotive scene.

You firstly need to decide what your character's Initial and Effective emotions are.

We'll look at a scene between Herman and Rhonda that takes place seven years after their marriage. The setting is their lounge room at home. We'll firstly look at it from the perspective of Rhonda.

Before the scene takes place the 'Given Circumstances' are:

Herman is not yet home from work, he was due one hour ago. Rhonda has made a wonderful surprise roast dinner that is getting dryer and dryer by the minute. It is their anniversary; Rhonda has been planning this special meal for the last month. There are candles on the table, soft music caresses the mildly scented room and a beautifully wrapped present sits lovingly on Herman's favorite chair. Rhonda is found sitting on a stool as the curtain goes up.

For this example we'll have Rhonda's Initial Emotion as 'Hurt', she has gone to a great deal of trouble and effort to prepare this meal and the lounge room for tonight, she feels hurt because Herman is still not home when he knows that it's their anniversary.

So, the first thing you need to find for your Emotional preparation is the feeling of 'hurt', your Initial Emotion.

Now because we generally protect our vulnerable Initial Emotions, Rhonda is going to create an Effective Emotional barrier of 'Anger'.

Rhonda will be angry because Herman has caused her to feel 'hurt'. So before the curtain goes up you get that deep sinking hurt feeling, once that Initial Emotion is firmly set, start 'dealing' with this hurt by projecting 'anger' towards your 'Other'. Because

Herman is not home yet, your current 'Other' would be in your imagination.

"When he gets home I'll ..."

Also, the settings and food that you have prepared will constitute 'Others'. As you look around the room you see constant reminders of the work and effort you have put in for this evening. This feeds your hurt, your anger. Your character has been stewing on this for about an hour.

The curtain goes up. You try not to be angry; you try to deal as effectively as you can. Suppressed anger shows on your face but as you look around the room the audience can see the work you've put in and the 'hurt' residing deep down. You engage in Behavior. Maybe you straighten the tablecloth. The sound of keys fitting into a door is heard; you jerk your head towards the door. Herman enters...

The creation and retention of your Emotional Preparation lasts for only the first moment of the scene. If your preparation is strong enough it will color everything that you do from then on. Don't hold onto the preparation, if you do you'll be acting from what you think your character should be feeling rather than what they are feeling. Stay connected to your 'Others' and allow them to move and effect you. Maybe in the Rhonda/Herman saga you'll get angrier, maybe you'll pacify a bit, maybe you'll get back onto your Initial emotion and feel hurt, find out during the performance.

The director will have given you guide posts for the direction that they would like the scene to head. If you find that you are straying too far off their plan then you need to honestly cue, in the moment, a behavior and response that will get it 'back-on-track'. You do this by re-labeling the physiological arousal that underpins your current emotional state.

So let's say that Herman's big brown puppy dog eyes have gotten the better of you; you are starting to calm down after barraging him with abuse. Now the director wants the scene to end at a highly emotional state of anger so that when we see you and Herman again in a couple of scenes time, snuggling, having just had sex, the comedy is heightened. What you would need to do is find a real cue onto which you can label that anger. Maybe you remember the roast still in the oven, burnt to a crisp; maybe you cue anger off the fact that his big brown eyes always soften you up; whatever it is it needs to be real in that moment for a 'truthful' performance to take place.

There are a couple of main ways that I prepare an emotional state before a scene. The first way requires a book of its own and as such I will leave it until I can do it justice. However, the other way is very effective and is expanded upon below.

## Phrase Prepping

Phrase Prepping sees you choosing an emotionally significant phrase that underlies your initial emotion at the start of the scene. For example your partner may have asked to talk with you about something "serious". You may be bracing yourself for the news that they want to separate. Your Prep Phrase may be "I love you." In an ideal situation your partner would also have a Prep Phrase. Theirs may be something like, "I'm so sorry". You and your scene partner would then connect with each other and, in turn, state your Prep Phrase. The important thing is to make sure that you get *'through'* to the other person. Genuinely connect and effect them with your phrase. You and your partner repeat the phrases until you feel there is an honest connection; you then start the dialogue riding the connection that you have formed. After the scene commences allow the emotion to evolve wherever it goes as a result of being connected in the moment. This is a very successful preparation method which I use ALL the time. I can't recommend it highly enough.

If you wish to Phrase Prep without the other actor using this method, simply connect with them before the scene and say your line in your head. This is harder but often the most practical given that usually the other actor will not work this way.

## Intellectual Preparation

Your Intellectual preparation should set up your 'head space' before going into the performance; it should focus your mind on who you are and what you want.

During the course of researching your character you should find three to five short statements about who you, your character, thinks they are. These are defining statements for your character. Begin each statement with, I am, the first statement should always be your character's name:

For example:

"I am Robyn Simpson."
"I am very intelligent."
"I am intolerant of any injustice in the world."
"I am always there to help anyone in trouble."

These lines focus your mind on who you are and prepare you to live that life. Add one final line which you will repeat over and over until you start the scene. This is, of course, your Prep Phrase.

Keep your focus on your 'Other'.

As you recite the statements allow them to effect you; Effect your body posture, your personal space, your vulnerability, take the feeling into your body and live inside it.

*Quick Summary*

So, before your performance you should:

1) Address any spiritual elements if necessary.
2) Physically warm-up and stretch your body.
3) Warm-up vocally.
4) Prepare your emotional state.
5) Recite your character statements.

## Emotionally Charging Props

We first looked at Emotionally Charged Props in Chapter 3, now we'll look at how you actually do that.

Let's say that you are going to be playing the role of 'Bob' in an upcoming film. You may remember that Bob was our high-flying executive in Chapter Five. Last time we saw him, Bob was defending himself from Luke, the country born lad whose pig farm was right next door to a proposed nuclear waste-dumping site to be created by Bob's company.

Earlier in the film is a scene depicting Bob's graduation ceremony from University. In this scene he is given a golden pen with his name engraved on one side and on the other the words, 'Love First'. His Grandmother, as a graduation present, gives this pen to him. Bob and his Grandmother are very close; he spent many a school holiday with her on a small sheep farm out west.

Bob's grandmother instilled many of his values in him, one of which was that in times of trouble and turmoil or when you don't know what to do, always remember that 'love comes first'.

Following the Graduation Scene are many more scenes depicting Bob and his career as he moves up the corporate ladder. Bob quickly finds himself caught up in the dog-eat-dog world of the big multi-nationals.

Which brings us to a moment near the end of the film when final negotiations are completed over the nuclear waste site and all that is needed is his signature and the deal is done. Bob pulls out his golden pen and holds it poised ready to sign. Bob's eyes fall upon the words, 'Love First'. He sees all the businessmen and women standing around him, dollars in their eyes; he remembers Luke, Jessie-May and all the town folk from his visit to the site. He remembers the pre-school and the nursing home. He remembers his grandmother...

So for Bob this pen has an emotional history with him, it is a tie into who he is and where he has come from. Now you the actor, for the film, need to charge this pen emotionally, it should have a connection with you rather than just being a prop handed to you before the next take.

If this was a decent budget film then you could probably ask to have an identical pen made for yourself to use. On a very low budget film you may just have to go out and get one made for yourself. At any rate a good idea is to get a copy of the one that will be used.

Hopefully during the shooting schedule, the graduation ceremony will be shot before the scene of potential signing. (Films are very rarely shot in order) If this is the case then the actual ceremony scene will give you one historical encoding memory with the pen.

Because the pen represents much more than merely a writing implement, the use of Imaginative Visualization with your Grandmother, coupled with Transference of Effect, will imbue the pen with an emotional tie to your Grandmother.

In the film the actress playing your Grandmother is in only a few scenes, these include the graduation ceremony and some nostalgic flashbacks. As such you may not have time to adequately explore your relationship with her. So what you'll need are a few things to help.

Photographs are always a good visual stimulus for this situation. If you can get some photos of her, these would be handy. Put one in your wallet to look at during the course of the day, another in your bedroom and maybe one on the wall at home. Get used to seeing her face, in particular see her face with the pen. Leave the pen next to a photo of your character's grandmother on your desk at home or some other place you frequent. This means that the pen and grandmother are being encoded together.

## *Recovery*

An actor who recovers well can take the biggest risks. While it may be wonderful for you to experience real emotions on stage or screen, it is equally important that you know how to recover from them. Likewise if you are having emotional problems in your own life, you need ways of dealing with them so that they don't effect your performances.

The process of recovery utilizes a combination of both your intellect and your emotions and is seeded within the Interaction Model.

If you go through all the stages of the Interaction, maintaining your initial emotion, then recovery is not an issue; a completed Interaction is self-recovering. However if you get stuck in a stage, or don't progress through to the Commitment Stage using the Initial Emotion then you may need to consciously recover.

How do we do that? Simply, but not easily. By consciously moving ourselves through the five stages of Interaction we will complete the recovery.

You may have little episodes from your life that occasionally spring into your consciousness and cause you discomfort. Generally they are 'negative' feelings in that they elicit emotions that you'd rather not have. These little episodes contain unresolved emotions stemming from your inability at the time to complete the interaction with your Initial Emotion.

**A hypothetical example:**

When you were at school years ago, during a lunch break, some-one came up from behind while you were talking to some girls, one of which you really liked, and pulled your pants down leaving nothing to their imagination.

The most likely reason that this was an unresolved interaction is that not only did you not go through your initial emotion of embarrassment, instead re-labeling to anger and chasing the culprit, but you also did not fully accept what happened.

## *Intellectual Method for Recovery*

First you need to get yourself into a good state of relaxation, this will be addressed later in this Chapter. Once in a relaxed state you take yourself back to the time and place of the event in your imagination. When the incident occurs you enter 'First Contact'. Then, to get into the next stage, you need to realize **and accept** what has happened. You need to say to yourself;

"I was naked in front of all those girls, they saw everything, there is nothing that I can do about it, it has happened and nothing will change that. How do I feel? I feel hurt, I feel embarrassed." Allow yourself to feel the hurt, the embarrassment, make noises out loud if you need to, cry if it effects you that way, just allow whatever comes up, to come up. Once you have embraced the initial emotion, fully experiencing it until it naturally subsides, and have also realized and accepted what has happened, you now need to enter the next stage - **'Need'**.

What do you need? Well, you are probably feeling very vulnerable and hurt and so need to feel safe. Acknowledge this to yourself. "I need to be safe". Next you enter the Evaluation Stage. What are you going to do about it? "How am I going to be safe?" Since you can't change the past you can either keep dredging it up or you can accept it, learn from it and get on with your life. You don't have to like what has happened just accept. So you now decide that you'll go and have a double chocolate sundae and put it all behind you.

If you have been successful in each stage then the emotive episode will no longer haunt you. You may remember it from time to time, but it will no longer hold the emotional sting that it has in the past.

This recovery isn't just for episodes in the past; you may use it for something that has happened recently. This is a good way of dealing with issues that may effect your focus during a performance or class.

If the situation is one that needs to be dealt with in the future then use the Thought Vault.

## The Thought Vault

The Thought Vault sees you writing down all of your thoughts on the subject of concern. By putting your thoughts, worries and concerns on paper you free up your mind to focus on your acting, happy in the knowledge that you can come back to the dilemma later on. You won't forget the important points as they are safely written down and stored in your Thought Vault.

## Practical Exercises

Use the monologue that you learned in the last Chapter as a practice text for your Preparations. Do the five steps - 1) Address any spiritual elements if necessary. 2) Physically warm-up and stretch your body. 3) Warm-up vocally. 4) Prepare your emotional state. 5) Recite your character statements. Once you have done these, launch into performance. Try numerous different Prep Phrases, have fun discovering the variety of meanings that may be gleaned from the script.

# CHAPTER 8

# *Putting it all Together*

```
Ahhh...
```

## Introduction

This is the final Chapter and probably the easiest and most relaxed. In this section you are going to take a journey from script to performance, just to get an overview on how it all fits together.

By now you've probably realized many more implications and uses for the various concepts that have been presented. My hope is that you will discover what works for you and evolve your acting style around your previous and future knowledge. You will find uses and ways of working with the 'Carne Method' that I haven't even considered, mainly because of your unique background and other training. I want you to be a thinking, working actor. You need to push yourself to discover, to explore, to learn more about acting ... you need to work!

But enough of the future, let's now look at Putting it all Together.

## The Script

The first thing you need to do is to read the script and do a basic analysis. In **Chapter 6** there is a section titled **'Confronting a Script'** which you should follow. Once you have completed that you next need to expand upon the 'given' to flesh out the life of your character.

## Character History

You now need to start thinking about filling in the gaps in your characters history, details concerning their lives that you don't find in the script but are relevant to information contained therein. For example, you may hate dogs but it is never spelt out in the script as to why. Make up a reason that fits in with the script, ie, when you were five you were watching A Current Affair on TV and saw a story on dogs that had mauled people. Had a nightmare that night. Scared of them ever since. This information informs you as an actor and informs the behavior that you have when seeing or talking about dogs.

Once you have filled in the gaps, set about writing your full character history. Expand on themes in the script and fill out their life details to get a full portrait of the character you will be playing. This background may be as brief or extensive as you like, depending on the size of the role and what **you** in particular need to bring this unique character to life. If the role is very small you may only need a couple of paragraphs. If the role is a lead in a feature film then it may be several pages long.

Again it all depends on you, this is your way of working that you are evolving so whatever you end up doing needs to work for you!

## Causal Chains

Isolate any relevant causal chains that may have an effect on your character's decisions. Examine any major decisions that your character makes and create a history for them, stepping-stones to their current decision.

For example you may play a character who, at the very start of the film, shoots a man with a pistol. There are many, many visual and auditory clues that will inform the audience about the character. If the character is male, wears a dark suit, shows no emotional investment in the act, and calmly puts the pistol away as he walks over to his black BMW and drives away, immediately the audience has a 'feel' for the character. The 'feel' would be much different if the character was female, her hands shaking, ripped dress and hair everywhere as she points the gun at a man ushering a young girl into the back of his panel van!

For the moment let's assume that the script gives us no clues as to the background of the later example. As the actor, to aid in your preparation, a chain of events that leads up to this big event will help greatly in your performance. Your chain of events may go something like this. (Remember, this chain may be more fully fleshed out and enhanced in the full character history)

**(PENNY)**
Happy Childhood - Father dies - Mother works hard, lonely, going is tough - Mother meets Man - Mother is raped by Man, you are 8yrs old, you see it happen - Mother goes into her shell - You look after Mother as best you can - You both get evicted from Flat as you can't meet the bills - Mother is found dead.

You go into foster-care - Loving family who live on a small farm - You learn to shoot a gun in the back paddock, firing at old cans.

You finish school and go to college - You get teased at College as frigid, sex is something you do not participate in - One night, while walking across campus, some guys grab you and take you into the dark. They start undressing you, you manage a scream before they muffle your mouth - A passing Lecturer hears you and saves you just in time - You are a wreck - your grades fall and you drop out of college.

You become paranoid, sleeping with a gun under your pillow and carrying one with you at all times - An old friend from college invites you out, she cares about you and wants to help - You go out dancing one night - Late in the evening some drunk guys try to hit on you and your friend - You react instinctively and slap one across the face - He calls you a bitch and grabs you, ripping your dress in the exchange - He throws you to the ground and they leave - Your friend checks if you are alright, you reassure her before she goes to the bathroom, when she returns you have left.

You wander the streets, eyes red, you clutch a necklace that your mother gave you – you wander – then you see him, the man who raped your mother, he is ushering a small girl about eight years old into the back of a panel van, your hands are trembling – you take your gun out of your bag and shoot.

By creating a background you have a wealth of information to draw your performance from. No longer are you just a two-dimensional figure; you are a living, breathing human with a history, a history that effects your decisions in the moment.

## *Sociological Spheres of Influence*

What are your characters' Sociological Spheres of Influence? Make a list of all the relevant social groups that your character associates with. How do these Spheres of Influence effect your characters perceptions and decision-making?

In our example with Penny some of her Spheres of Influence include; Natural family, Foster Family, School and College. Throughout the script you may discover more but we'll just have a look at those for now.

Penny's Natural family was very loving and caring, Father dies, this changes the home environment, now her Mother has all the responsibilities; Mother is raped and withdraws into herself, Penny's home environment changes again; Penny's Mother dies, another change in home environment.

How did each of these changes effect her? How do those environments effect her perceptions and decision-making? What was her school environment like? Who were her friends and what were their interests?

The College environment would greatly effect her. Did she belong to any groups? Drama club, swimming club, chess club??? When she was nearly raped at College, did that change her Spheres of Influence or decision-making? Maybe that night she was on her way back from a club meeting, she may have given up that club to avoid the walk home in future. Her decisions about going out at night may have changed. Her Spheres of Influence change, as does her Behavior.

If she was coming back from Karate club her perception of the situation, and her Behavior, may have been different than if she was on her way back from the sewing club.

Look closely at your character's Spheres of Influence and see how they affect behavior, perceptions and decision making.

## Trust

Are there any references to Trust in the script? Do they trust Behaviorally, Unconditionally, somewhere in between or in some other way?

In the example of Penny, she may have lost all behavioral trust in males. Maybe she is very selective of who she trusts. Even then she may be very guarded about who she lets get close to her, females included. Perhaps the only one she really trusts, unconditionally, is her Foster Mother who used to hold her at night, wipe her tears and love her unconditionally.

## Vulnerability

What Vulnerability traits does your character generally display? When do they go against their normal Vulnerabilities? Are they normally Socially or Personally Vulnerable? Are they Emotionally or Intellectually Vulnerable? Why? Use this information to generalize their likely behavior in imaginary circumstances. Internalize these vulnerabilities so when performing they will influence your Behavior without thinking.

Using our example, what do you think Penny's vulnerabilities may be? For the moment let's call her Emotionally/Socially Vulnerable. (This is not definitively right or wrong, just my choice for this example)

Her Emotional Vulnerability has stemmed from her loving mother figures and the fact that she is well educated which will enhance the Intellectual Barriers. Most of her childhood hurt has been meticulously buried deep down, only to surface in the form of some subtle, and some, not-so-subtle neuroses.

There are some things that she finds very hard to Intellectualize, these things break through her Intellectual barriers and force her into her Emotional/Physical Vulnerabilities. Physical abuse and dominant males crash their way through her barriers, she cries, she slaps faces, she fires guns.

Because of her problems socially, particularly with men, she tends to be a bit of a loner. She deals effectively on her own and is withdrawn in social environments.

## Personal Space

What is your character's 'Normal' Personal Space? If they were brought up in the country they are likely to have a large personal space, in the city would generally mean a smaller area. Are they interacting with people who have a personal space vastly different to their own? What does this mean? How might this effect your character? Internalize so it again becomes automatic in performance.

Where might Penny's Personal Space be? She lived in a city environment until the age of nine; thereafter was raised by her foster parents on a small farm.

Remember there is no definitive right or wrong in any characterization, just the way that you'd like to play them.

For our example we are going to have Penny as having a large Personal Space around people that she doesn't know, particularly men, and a small personal space around those whom she trusts. From this we can get an idea of how she'll interact at the Police station after she's caught.

She may be more comfortable with female police officers than male and may even get violent if a police**man** tries to touch her. Or she could retreat her Personal Space further and go into Withdrawn Imagination, curling up in a ball in the corner of her cell, gently rocking backward and forward. She may even '*break*', if she can no longer find protection in her imagination she may become totally vulnerable and allow anything to happen to her. In this instance she will have given up totally on herself, no longer holding any value on her body, mind or soul. If she cared just a little bit more, she may even hang herself...

## Items

Are there any items relevant to your character that you can obtain and emotionally charge? What do these items mean to your character? Are they a part of your own characters unique persona or do they fit in with one of their Sociological Spheres of Influence? Maybe it's a pendant that all members of a particular gang wear, or maybe it's your Grandmothers' wedding ring given to you in her Will.

In our example there is one salient Item that Penny owns and that is a necklace given to her from her maternal mother. When you are playing Penny this necklace may be used as a wonderful emotional link to your mother and who you are.

There may be set behavior around this necklace. Perhaps every night when Penny is going to sleep, she places it on a pillow beside the bed. When she gets stressed she may clutch at the necklace, seeking support and comfort.

With the emotional charging of this item, we see potentials within the interaction. What happens at the Police Station if she has to take all her jewelry and personal items off and leave them with a male officer? What does it mean to her to not have the necklace? What does it mean to give it to a man? Is the non-possession of the necklace the final straw that breaks her?

### *Status*

What do you see as your character's general Status in relationship to the other characters, both in Interactional Status and Social Status? Who do you think may be higher or lower than you? Why? Remember these are only perceptual guesses the actual status will be found in the moment; this information informs your performance as to the status that you will make a bid for.

So far with our 'Penny' example, we have seen this character as progressively deteriorating in mental and physical strength. Her Personal Space barriers expanding as she has been getting more desperate.

Let's turn that on its head! Let's say that after Penny shot the man she suddenly found a strength and power that she had never felt before. Suddenly she can control a situation, suddenly she isn't the weak one, and suddenly she can make a difference. She feels the power, no one can hurt her now! Her status rises.

Penny goes to the Police Station, the police handle her roughly, she doesn't care, they can't hurt her. She feels complete; the man who took her mother and life away from her is dead, by her hand! They ask her why she did it, she doesn't **need** to answer, she doesn't need to tell them anything, she smiles and her status rises. The frustration shows on the police's faces, they confirm their lower status. They put the heavy word on her, trying to raise their own status, trying to get her to talk. They fail.

## Interaction

Does your character tend to dwell in any one particular area of the Interaction? If so, what does this mean physically and behaviorally for your character? What are the Status, Vulnerability and Personal Space implications of them dwelling predominantly in the area? Allow all this information to effect your written history of the character. Make specific notes on Personal Space, Vulnerabilities, etc.

For Penny, is there any one particular area that she predominantly dwells? Before the shooting we may place her primarily in Evaluation, after the shooting, Realization/Acceptance. We looked at her status rising in the last section with the Realization of power and strength. What if after she shot the man she never entered the Realization/Acceptance Stage? What if she got stuck in First Contact? If we go with this scenario then Penny is in shock, her body weight and vocal quality both up, eyes wide. Everything is a bit like a dream.

*"There's a man lying on the ground covered in red stuff. He really doesn't look well. And here comes a nice policeman, he's quite cute. Oh, I get to ride in the police car! Can we put the siren on? Where's mum? I can't wait to tell her I got a ride in a police car. She will be so proud!"*

So for your character see if there is one particular area of the interaction that you may center them in. This area may change at times, marking a different stage for your character.

## Other Thoughts on Written History

Make your written history as detailed or brief as you like. It is up to you, whatever works. My character backgrounds are generally a few pages long. This gives me scope to define the behavioral background to their idiosyncrasies and to breathe the first rays of light into a 'real' person. Things I also generally include are;

Happiest memory.
Saddest memory.
First love.
A birthday party experience.
Family experiences.

Basically anything that I feel will help to inform my performance, and anything relevant to the script. I like to make mine quite comical, this is not necessary but I enjoy it more and consequently find that I use it more. It also helps to free the mind and so I find that I'm more relaxed and creative.

## *Learn Your Lines*

As soon as possible, LEARN YOUR LINES!!! Make sure that you know them almost as well as you know the alphabet. It is not enough to know them *well*, they must be recollected without the slightest hesitation. Also make certain that you don't memorize your lines in any specific way. You need to learn them constantly, CONNECTED TO THE 'OTHER', as per **Chapter 6**. Don't forget to change your 'Other' all of the time; basically you are improvising behavior around set dialogue. Be careful not to encode lines with any particular emphasis, this will only serve to keep you from being actually connected **'now'** with the 'Other' in performance, in the moment!

## Research

Do some research on your character. If your character is in jail, try to visit a jail. If your character likes bowling, go bowling. If your character is a street alcoholic, go to a park and watch a few of them. Find people like your character. Go where they go. Watch them closely. Look at their behavior, their status, and their personal space. See what they to do to deal with their environment. People do things to be comfortable. How do they get comfortable? Physically? Emotionally? Intellectually? Spiritually?

## Script Analysis

If you wish to formally break the script into beats or 'bits', then do that, also you might like to look at Set-up and Target dialogue. Remember only use these when they will help: It's **your** acting style, **your** choice. I use them occasionally, every script is different, every character unique, find what works for your specific circumstance.

## Preparation

As per **Chapter 7** in the **Intellectual Preparation** section, find yourself five or so short statements about who you, your character, thinks they are. Read and re-read your character notes. Vulnerabilities, History etc.

Work out the Emotional Preparation that you'll need for each scene. In our example, what might be your preparation for Penny just before the director calls 'Action' for her shooting the man scene? Some possible Preparations might be;

      I am Penny Moss
      I love my mother
      I am scared of men
      I need to feel safe

I have had enough of running!
I am going to kill you.

On the emotional side you may want to prepare for an Initial Emotion of 'Fear'. On seeing the 'man' you may re-label the 'Fear' to 'Anger' that becomes your effective emotion. The audience will see the truly **Great Actor** when they see a very scared little girl, within an angry external adult.

So, before you go into the scenes, do all your preparations, as per **Chapter 7**, and have fun!

## *Chapters Interacting*

With the 'Carne Method', you now have a foundation template in which you can incorporate new information and techniques on acting. The Interaction is at the core of the method. Vulnerability, Status and Personal Space satellite the Interaction, all aspects effecting each other. Look closely at the following diagram; it summarizes the key elements of the method. Use it as a reference for future integration of other theories and techniques.

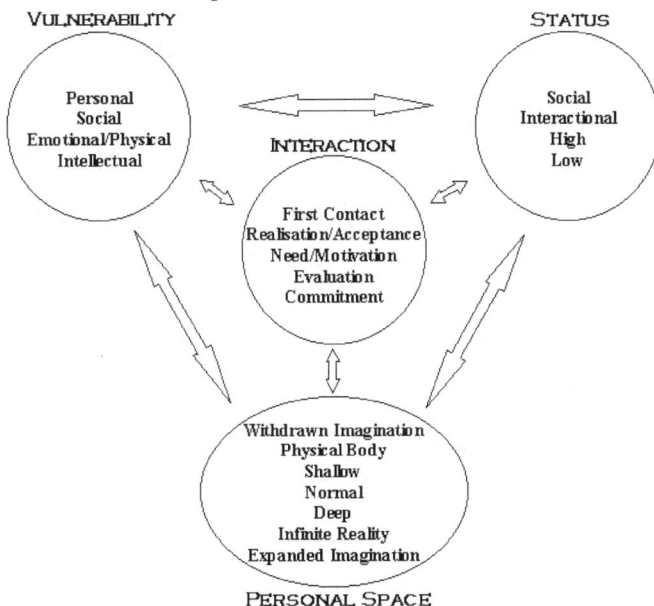

```
        VULNERABILITY                              STATUS

        ┌──────────┐                           ┌──────────┐
        │ Personal │                           │  Social  │
        │  Social  │    ⇐═══════⇒              │Interactional│
        │Emotional/Physical│   INTERACTION     │   High   │
        │Intellectual│                         │   Low    │
        └──────────┘                           └──────────┘
                    ⇖         ┌──────────┐        ⇗
                              │First Contact│
                              │Realisation/Acceptance│
                              │Need/Motivation│
                              │ Evaluation │
                              │ Commitment │
                              └──────────┘
                                   ⇕
                         ┌──────────────────┐
                         │Withdrawn Imagination│
                         │  Physical Body   │
                         │     Shallow      │
                         │      Normal      │
                         │       Deep       │
                         │  Infinite Reality│
                         │Expanded Imagination│
                         └──────────────────┘
                           PERSONAL SPACE
```

*Robert Carne*
## Things to Remember

When you are performing always stay **connected to the 'Other'**.

**Your preparation only lasts the first moment of the scene**, allow your 'Other/s' to constantly have an effect on you, changing the emotional journey in-the-moment.

It's not necessarily the emotion that you show that's interesting; **it's the emotion that you're trying NOT to show** that will hold an audience.

At a pivotal moment when your barriers are breached and your Initial Emotion is displayed, does your character allow themselves the vulnerability or do they try to rebuild their walls?

**Keep breathing**. Holding your breath will only stop your creativity and 'truth'.

**Act with your whole body**. Find the Behavior that helps your character to get comfortable, to 'deal' effectively with the situation.

**Have fun!**

Always be **relaxed** when performing. Even though your character may be tense, the actor should be relaxed.

**Love** every character you play.

**Preparation** is 90% of a successful performance.

You can use the physiological arousal from stage fright to fuel your Initial Emotion in performance.

Allow **non-dialogue sounds** (gutturals) to come naturally while connected to the 'Other'.

It is important that the audience **'cares'** about your character. They may love them, or hate them, but if they don't 'care' then there is no theatrical point to their existence.

Keep a firm focus on your 'Other', if you fidget or look away this will scatter the focus, hold eye contact. What are they feeling is more important than what you are feeling. Your emotion will be a result of them.

## Final Words

Well, that's it for now. Well done! I have a few final thoughts I'd like to share with you and also some words of thanks to some instrumental people in my life.

Now listen very closely my brave dedicated student. If you want to be an actor, if that is truly where you get the most joy and nothing else will suffice. Then do it! Don't make excuses for yourself, work hard and keep going. Anything is possible.

**Don't pursue it as a dream, pursue it as a reality!**

Make it your reality! Be a generous actor, a giving actor, and an actor that other actors want to work with. You must treat every character with love and care. You are portraying aspects of humanity to the local community or to the world, treat them with respect and professionalism.

I know that you may have had people laugh at you for wanting to be an actor. Maybe your parents tried to dissuade you from doing it.

*"Get a real job"*
*"You have to have something to fall back on"*
*"Be Realistic"*

And so on, yes I've heard them all too!

I remember many years ago I was talking with my voice coach and he told me a story about something that had happened to him a few years previously. He said that he was at a party and for one reason or another found himself sitting under a table with another actor. They were talking. The actor said to him words to the effect, "I'm thinking about giving it away, I don't know if I'm good enough, it's such a hard industry I'll never make it". That actor was Mel Gibson.

Let me give you realistic. **You may be hit by a bus tomorrow!** Most people live their lives, never pursuing their true loves. Most people have regrets about their lives. "If only I had..." Assuming you only get one crack at life, make the most of it! There is a price that you will need to pay for success, pay it! (Please don't compromise your morals in the process, you don't need to).

Find your way into the industry. You may write, direct and act in your own short films. You may go to a major Acting School and get an agent. You may become a wealthy Entrepreneur and fund your own films. You might become a director or acting coach. Keep trying to find ways in, keep acting, and keep learning.

Sometimes the price you can pay is financial. Maybe you will have to get a 'no-brainer' job to be able to afford to eat and take classes. In the end analysis if the price for your acting success, what ever that may be, is too high for you, then don't pay it. I know this seems to contradict what I've said previously but if there are other things that are more important, then do whatever, as long as it is your decision and you are happy with it. You may decide that you just want acting as a hobby. That is totally fine; enjoy it. This is your life make the most of it. The low points for an actor can be very low, but the high points... WOW!

One word of advice when looking for a 'no-brainer' job; Obviously keep studying acting and creating your own work but **try to get a job in the industry**. Tearing tickets at a cinema, ushering at a theatre, sweeping stage floors whatever. But try, try, try to stay in touch with the industry at all times. Make the industry a part of your life, even if it isn't as the lead in an international blockbuster… for now…

Once again, thank you for taking this journey; I hope you have enjoyed it. I wish you all the best for a wonderful, loving and fruitful life.

*Robert Carne*
## Thank you

A big **THANKS** to Anthony Bova! Anthony owns 'Spartan Health' a fantastic health program and is a close personal friend. Thanks to all my family & friends for their love and support. Special thanks to Sally McDonald for her particular support in this project.

Thanks to my wonderful, wonderful parents for all their support over the years and a big thanks to Tanya for her support and for the wonderful stretching pictures contained within. Thanks to my darling daughter Tiana, the wonderful Caroline and the amazing Linde all very special ladies in my life.

I'd like to thank the Goodwin-Ward family for their love and support over the years. I think of you as family and love you all dearly.

And finally thank you to you. One of my most recent of students, may all your realities come true.

## Practical Exercises

Go over everything in this book; make it a part of you. See the world through actor's eyes. Keep up the practical exercises throughout this course.

Watch movies and Theatre productions; make sure you keep breathing and not holding your breath. This is an excellent way of keeping in touch with your Initial Emotion. Allow yourself to feel. Great actors don't **make** themselves feel a strong emotion; great actors **allow** themselves to feel it.

Go and take some classes. Seek out good acting coaches. If you are not happy with one acting coach, go and find another. If you feel you have gained all you can from one person, move on. Keep learning. Use what works for you and leave what doesn't. Any Acting Coach that tells you that they have **THE** answer is kidding themselves, run!

Get involved in productions. Do as much acting as you can. Start your own work. Make short films using a video camera. Find other like-minded people to work with. Live as an actor.

Talk about acting. Do short courses. Be a student of human Behavior.

When you feel confident, get a Theatrical Agent. Be very wary of newspaper advertisements there are a lot of rip-offs out there. The best way to find a good agent is to watch in the credits of films and TV shows that you like, see who casts them, and then ring them up and ask which agents they deal with. This way you know that your agent is genuine and gets work.

Make a list of all the things that you want to achieve in acting. Make a list of all the things that you are going to do to make the things you want happen for you, ie, the stepping stones to your goals. Order the lists into one causal chain that starts with the very first thing you need to do and culminates in your end goal.

Finally... **Do the List!**

# Appendix A

## *Sanford Meisner's Repetition Exercise*

Sanford Meisner was truly one of the greatest Acting coaches of the 20$^{th}$ Century. His techniques have survived the test of time and continue to enjoy a place within acting classes around the world to this day. I do not see this trend ending any time soon. Such was his Legacy to inform acting technique well into the future.

I never had the pleasure of attending one of his classes personally. I was originally introduced to his work in 1990 and it has made a huge impact on my approach to acting. Since then I have trained with numerous coaches who teach the 'Meisner' technique. Every one of them has taught it differently. While some may argue that this 'bastardization' of his technique is an horrendous injustice to the work, others see the Meisner technique as an evolving platform, morphing into whatever works for the unique practitioner. Some of my experiences with teachers of 'Meisner' have been inspirational, others less so. The inspirational ones truly understand how the exercise works for them.

I am about to go in to detail on the way I use Meisner's Repetition exercise. What follows is purely the theory underlying the way I use the exercise and I do not for a moment pretend that this reflects Meisner's intent. With all tribute paid to the great man, I hope you find something in the following for you.

### *Primary Function*

I see the primary function of the repeat exercise to bring participants into connection with their Initial Emotion and with their "Other". Once actors know and give themselves permission to experience their initial emotion, they may then use this 'truth' as a base upon which to build a character's Effective Emotion. In performance the Actor experiences their Initial Emotion and then, through character choice, protect that vulnerability with a character's Effective Emotion. This gives a three dimensional performance where, for example, an audience may see a character angry after losing a loved one but also view the underlying devastation through which the anger is born.

In order for an actor to get in touch with their Initial Emotion they must be put in a position where it is hard for them to re-label what they are feeling. Take away their capacity for evaluation and they will be forced back on to their Initial Emotion. If we look at the Interaction Model, the highest point of Initial Emotion is within the Need stage. This is where we want to get the actor, just before they hit Evaluation and proceed to intellectualize their Initial Emotion away.

The actor's physicality when in the Repeat exercise should be centered. An off-center physicality facilitates evaluation, as seen in the Evaluation Stage of the Interaction, keep the actor centered and it is harder for them to re-label their Initial Emotion.

Maintain eye contact. With the actors maintaining eye contact and 'connecting' the face takes up a significant amount of cognitive space. This capturing of 'thinking' space leaves them depleted on intellectual resources which could help them to get away from their Initial Emotion. And so, again, we see the capacity of the actor to escape to an Effective Emotion impaired.

And finally by continuing the repeat back and forth, and only changing the repeated phrase when something forces its way into consciousness, the 'brain space' available has become, for all intents and purposes, full.

All these aspects working together make it very hard for the actor to re-label their initial emotion. The actor is now exercising their initial emotion, getting in touch with their emotional instrument and broadening their performance scope.

## *The Repetition in Action*

When viewing the Repeat exercise there are tell tail signs when an actor is "in their head" or is feeling an Initial Emotion that they are trying to re-label away. Any off-center physicality, like leaning to the side or head tilted should tell the Acting coach that the student is seeking refuge in the Evaluation stage of the Interaction. Fidgeting feet, fingers moving, hands twitching, knees bobbing are all signs that a strong Initial Emotion is present and that the actor is trying desperately not to feel it.

In the Repeat exercise students should be in the "Deep" area of Personal Space. By pushing their personal space out over the other person to include their partner, the actors are becoming vulnerable and so the Initial Emotion is heightened.

Once actors are in tune consistently with their Initial Emotion it is then time to consider burying that emotion under a character's Effective Emotion in performance.

## *Taking the Repeat into Performance*

Actors need to trust their instincts. Reacting with a fabricated emotion, behaviour or line recitation from an idea of what you 'think' is happening, rather than simply instinctively reacting as a result of being connected to your 'Other' in the moment, will see a calculated performance that doesn't 'ring true'. The Repetition exercise hones 'connection' skills so that you may be fully available to respond to a 'real & present' cue from your 'Other'. It is the connection to your 'Other', in collaboration with your connection to the dialogue, which will define the Character within the performance. The character is defined in-the-moment, not from a pre-determined idea of who you think the character is. Allow yourself to respond without judgment in whichever manner your instincts dictate and a truly spontaneous and in-the-moment performance will be created.

Once you have your lines memorized and have done your scene preparation, as outlined earlier, take the connection of the Repetition exercise (not the physicality) into the scene. One of two things will happen. Either you allow your initial emotion to guide your instincts and performance or you drop an effective emotion on top of your honest initial emotion. For example; You are playing Herman & the director tells you;

"When you first see Boris with the knives, I want you to be frozen with fear. However, when Boris starts approaching you I want you to be enraged and move towards him".

In this instance the most likely initial emotion to emerge would be fear. However, once Boris starts advancing towards you, allow this behaviour of Boris to anger you. Rage is cued off your 'Other'. The fear will be relabeled and rage, born of fear will emerge. It is with this rage that you now advance towards Boris, allowing yourself to subsequently evolve in any direction as a result of your connection to Boris, your 'Other'.

As you are connected in-the-moment during the rehearsal process, potentials for moments will arise as you explore your character. Those potentials that instinctively feel right will be more likely to occur during a performance, while those that don't sit well will fall by the wayside. In this way the character will develop organically throughout rehearsals. Remember, just because a moment has 'worked' in the past doesn't mean that the dynamic will be present in any specific performance for it to work again. The actor must trust themselves and go with the moment, whether they have delivered similarly in the past or not. Don't plan responses, evolve as the scene dictates.

The emotional freedom that the Repetition exercise gives the actor is one of the greatest tools an actor may acquire.

Made in the USA
Lexington, KY
27 February 2013